VOGUE
ENTERTAINING

VOGUE
ENTERTAINING

WW

WestWind Publishers Inc.

Special Canadian Westwind Edition
published November 1988 in conjunction with
Shoppers Drugmart/Pharmaprix

Westwind Publishers
225 Duncan Mill Road
Don Mills, Ontario
M3B, 3K9

Printed by Mandarin Offset in Hong Kong

Text and photographs supplied by Vogue Australia

Vogue Australia Editor-in-chief June McCallum
Vogue Entertaining Guide Editor Carolyn Lockhart
Food Editor Joan Campbell

CONTENTS

INTRODUCTION

Welcome to *Vogue Entertaining*, a book as unique as the best-selling magazine that prompted it. All the material contained here has been taken from the highly successful *Australian Vogue* Entertaining Guide, a quarterly publication that features both home cooks and professionals who are renowned for the extraordinary prowess and finesse with which they entertain. Their love of food and natural approach to cooking is one that translates effortlessly to any country in the world and all the recipes in this book have been fully adapted to suit American ingredients and conditions.

The *Australian Vogue* editors and these talented home cooks have created beautifully balanced menus suitable for all types of occasions ranging from casual winter lunches to glamorous evening dinners; from instant meals built around take-away or emergency shelf ingredients, to lazy summer picnics and barbecues. A short introduction to each menu sets the scene and gives you advice on the selection, preparation, cooking and presentation of the dishes.

Today's trend is towards a more relaxed style of entertaining. Many of the menus are geared towards alfresco eating. Dinner becomes a moveable feast, the dining room is relocated in the garden, the verandah, the beach or the boat. Yet wherever the venue, the best of entertaining should have a simplicity about it that is by no means naive. The emphasis here is on selecting good quality, healthy ingredients that can be presented in an undisguised and unadulterated way, so that their true flavor and appearance can be fully appreciated.

A mingling of international culinary styles is another influence that has made an impression on today's approach towards entertaining around the world. Even everyday recipes have become far more cosmopolitan. South East Asia in particular has offered gastronomic inspirations which are now adopted by all Western countries. Japanese, Vietnamese, Indonesian and Thai cuisines are now as familiar as Chinese.

The recipes contained in *Vogue Entertaining* have been carefully selected, and most of them are designed to expand. Although some presuppose a basic knowledge of the principles of good cooking, they are well within the range of anyone with a love of good food and a willingness to have a try. Most recipes are photographed and we hope this will help the novice cook solve any presentation problems, or provide new ideas for the experienced cook.

We hope you will find *Vogue Entertaining* to be an exceptional guide to entertaining and an invaluable source of inspiration.

ENTERTAINING KNOW-HOW

When fresh air and sunshine are as natural as breathing, cooks rarely spend hours in the kitchen; therefore simplicity, speed and lightness are evident, in an approach that translates effortlessly to any country in the world. But with this lightness of touch there is a generosity of ingredients that has become a national trait.

All cuisines are constantly evolving. No country is afraid to take whatever it pleases from other areas of the world – the gusto of the Mediterranean, the spicy combinations of Asia – and make them peculiarly their own, as creative chefs have done throughout the ages.

The success of *Vogue Entertaining* has been that its recipes are gleaned from people in all walks of life; these are their longstanding favorites or their latest and most exciting discoveries.

The cooks, professional or private, whose recipes are revealed for you here, are nothing if not innovative. They seek freshness, spice and savor; even winter dishes are more inclined to be rich and robust in flavor than heavy in content. A love of food, we believe, does not mean over-indulgence at the table but a renewal of the spirits and a repast that rejuvenates; 'that which restores', is the true meaning of the word *restaurant*.

There is a huge variety of seafood, and an ever increasing range of fresh fruit and vegetables available. These foods feature largely on these pages, reflecting the trend towards healthier eating.

Whether you are a newcomer to the delights of successful entertaining, or an experienced cook looking for fresh ideas and inspiration, the pages of this book will be your guide.

The cookbook is grouped in sections to turn to at a glance: cooking for special occasions, alfresco informality, dinners with style, brunches and weekend meals, instant entertaining. Each section sets out a collection of menus planned to harmonize in flavor, with a balance of color, texture and theme; but each can be used just as successfully with others in this book.

Most recipes are simple, but in keeping with the *Vogue* philosophy of spontaneity, even those that require time in preparation and serving could be described as simple cooking in the grand manner. The sections range from lavish celebrations where time and skill are called for, to dinners on the run. On these occasions, remember to take a few moments to re-lax: speed in preparation should never carry over to the eating. If time for a meal is limited, the courses should be kept small and the food simple, with emphasis on fresh ingredients that aid digestion. Cream and rich ingredients should be kept to a minimum. Conversely, remember that sunshine and fresh air intensify the appetite noticeably.

The introduction to each section sets the scene and gives you more hints for each occasion.

Below: Sunny days lend themselves to alfresco entertaining. The effect need not be formal but it can look striking; an antique quilt covers this table and a selection of carved ducks adds an unexpected touch

In COME TO DINNER we show you how to entertain with *Vogue* style and elan. Some of the recipes in ENTERTAINING IN STYLE take time to prepare, but here it is assumed they will be planned for times when at least one extra pair of hands is taken for granted, THE LONG WEEKEND gives you a caché of recipes that are away from the run-of-the-mill and great thoughts for flexible brunches where pre-planning and a little advance preparation is the answer.

MORE TASTE THAN TIME gives you light and easy, carefree meals where organization is the key; a selection of ideas for the person who wants to serve something simple yet stylish and must do it with a minimum of fuss, in the least possible time – perhaps picking up last minute ingredients on the way home from the office.

ALFRESCO INFORMALITY shows you stylish additions to the American tradition of eating alfresco – barbecue and out-of-doors ideas that are far removed from the ordinary, and some indoor food that reacts deliciously to an added dash of sunshine – all to be served in the great outdoors: a country retreat, a boat or a tiny garden apartment or penthouse roof.

There are many ingredients to suc-

cessful entertaining, not least of them the personalities of the guests, but for the cook/host one simple rule almost guarantees success. Aim for balance: a balance of textures, flavors and color – for it is true that we eat with our eyes, and enjoyment is enhanced by meals that look as tantalizing as they taste. The key is to contrast and complement: a creamy soup followed by something to chew or crunch; a spicy dish before something bland; a rich main course followed by a crisp, light dessert. Nothing is more deadening to the taste buds than a flavor repeated too often, or dishes rich in cream from the beginning to the end of a meal.

When in doubt about what to serve for a dessert, fresh fruit at the peak of perfection presented on a bed of ice is always superb; if in a dilemma about vegetables, opt for a simple salad, always delicious. One *Vogue* editor suggests mastering, early in your career as an entertainer, the simple art of the soufflé. Individual soufflés, savoury or sweet, can be prepared ahead but for the last-minute cooking, and they never fail to create a sensation.

The menus that follow will give you a guide to perfect recipe balance. Study their harmonies. With practice, planning for a marriage of substance and flavor will become instinctive.

Develop a feel for ingredients. They vary enormously and behave differently at different times. For instance, herbs vary in intensity throughout the year. Recipes are not infallible; there are variables – atmospheric conditions, the quality of the basic ingredients, such as eggs and flour. Final results will vary and often it is not incorrect quantities or inaccurate measuring that is at fault but the behavior of the ingredients themselves. Consider the temperature – of the oven, the weather; even the cook's own body heat makes a difference. For instance, hot hands make tough pastry. Develop your senses, a feel for texture, a taste for compatible flavours, a smell for the pungency of herbs, an eye for top quality. Trust your instincts and resurrect your disasters. Some of the culinary greats were meant to be something else (roquefort, tarte tatin). Pure technical excellence often produces boring, predictable food. Be innovative and imaginative, and don't let a recipe – even the superb recipes here – dictate its terms. Observe the basic rules and then flout convention. Nothing replaces practice and experience, but the love of food is the most important ingredient you have.

As one of the contributors to this book says, 'There's only one great food style and that's the freshest ingredients used seasonally and served cleanly and beautifully.'

This fresh style of eating is enriching, not limiting. Any extra effort goes into the planning, not the cooking, and the benefits in health and vitality are welcome rewards.

Even the elaborate meals here are simple in each step of their preparation. Ease of entertaining is the aim, where the one who prepares the food not only appears to be but actually is enjoying the occasion. The basis of successful entertaining is being prepared. Organization is the key and that doesn't mean precooking. There's been a subtle shift in emphasis from cooking to planning ahead: doing your homework, knowing where to buy the freshest pasta at the last minute, finding the produce market that stays open late and having a plan of action in all departments, whether it is keying the whole dinner to a theme or trying out new recipes when you have the time, even if they are fast-cooked on the actual day.

Having the basic ingredients on hand is also important: reduced stocks, herb butters, homemade ice creams; improvize with garnishes, but keep them to a minimum – edible, relating to the dish, never overdone.

Above: Be adventurous, these striking colors sit together in perfect harmony

EMERGENCY SHELF

Behind every good cook is a good emergency shelf. Although we constantly reiterate that fresh is best, there are occasions – cooking for unexpected guests, days when there is no time to shop – when a cache of quality basics and specially prepared products can save the day.

Everyone's idea of the perfect standby ingredients will vary. However, it is advisable to think in terms of themes when stocking your pantry and group related items together to stimulate ideas for elegant, panic-free meals at short notice.

Italian food is always easy to prepare at the last minute and deliciously flavorful to serve when you have a good supply of relevant basics. Various types of pasta or Arborio rice provide the basis for your dinner. For sauces to be whipped up in minutes have on hand: canned, peeled whole tomatoes, tomato purée and paste, Parmesan cheese, garlic, oil, herbs, freshly ground pepper and rock salt. These make a good basic sauce. A can of baby clams in brine or anchovies in oil would make the sauce a little more special. Grissini sticks or black olives to serve as an accompaniment would enliven the dinner even further. For accompanying salads have: olives, sundried tomatoes, pimentoes, artichokes (*carciofini alla contadina*). A quick and delicious dessert can be made with amaretti or savoiardi cookies crushed and marinated in brandy and served with mascarpone cheese.

If Asian food is your speciality, think along these lines. Scour the Chinese produce stores for good quality, canned ingredients which make a delicious *salade composée*: lotus root, baby corn cobs, water chestnuts, Chinese quail eggs. To these, add salad vegetables in season and spice the vinaigrette with soy sauce. Other staples to give a meal an Asian flavor: hoi sin sauce, plum sauce and peanut oil to provide aromatic seasoning for ribs or pork.

You may be inspired to cook Japanese style if you have the following goods on hand: *Hiyamuji – Tsuyu* (soup base for noodles), Japanese noodles, red pickled ginger, *furikake* (seasoning mix for rice – hot, spicy, cod roe flavour) and *mirin* (natural sweet rice seasoning).

Other emergency shelf staples: vinegars, dried herbs, curry powders; freeze reductions of stocks, herb butters, homemade ice creams; have lemons on hand; grow your own herbs too, if possible, and a humble nasturtium plant in the garden will yield edible flowers and leaves.

Left: A platter of fresh fruit and cheese makes the perfect finale to any impromptu meal
Right: Break away from convention by using bold colors and original table decorations

TOOLS OF THE TRADE

Equipping a kitchen is as personal a matter as stocking your emergency shelf. While there are certain items which no aspiring or accomplished cook should be without, some equipment is useful only to the specialized cook. The best advice is to start with the basics, buying the best quality items you can as they will give better service in the long run.

The essentials include a set of good sharp knives and a knife sharpener or steel, good quality saucepans, a food processor, blender, a set of good quality mixing bowls – ideally dishwasher-proof; whisk, wooden spoons, baking pans and trays of many sizes, bread pans, colander, garlic press; a selection of large platters and baskets for serving and plastic air-tight canisters for storage.

In the handy, but non-essential category: a portable beater; a grinder for coffee and spices; a sifter; a wok; a mouli; mortar and pestle; an ice cream maker; a pasta-maker.

Obviously the amount and sophistic-ation of your equipment depends on how much cooking and entertaining you do and how much time you have. The career woman, wife and mother may wish to have all the electric gadgets she can find as her time undoubtedly will be in short supply. However, if the demands on your time are not so great, acquiring the latest in labor-saving equipment will not be a high priority. Just make sure that you have good quality essentials.

One word of advice: don't get carried away with the glamor of advertising and packaging. Sometimes bench and shelf space are more valuable than a mass of bulky electrical equipment. Ice cream makers are great if you make all your own ice cream, but not worthwhile if you only experiment with it two or three times a year.

WINES

wines before those at room temperature. A basic rule of thumb is to begin a meal with light, dry, chilled wines, and graduate to fuller, fruitier wines at room temperature as the meal progresses.

Once you have familiarized yourself with styles of wines, the best way to choose particular wines is to experiment. Taste and test (but not on your guests) and make notes for future reference so that you are confident about the wines which complement certain dishes.

However, the selection of wines is a very subjective matter, rather like choosing what to wear, and providing a harmonious marriage of food and wine is the important objective. Impressing guests with the age of a prized red is a useless exercise if the wine clashes with the food.

Certainly rules are made to be broken if the occasion warrants (for example, chilled red wine such as Beaujolais on a really hot day, Champagne throughout the meal), but, generally, wines should be appropriate to the time of year as well as the dish. In winter, for instance, a full-flavored white Burgundy may be a better choice than a delicate Rhine Riesling. The following is a guide only to the types of wines that are most suited to certain dishes.

Chilled, *good* Champagne always makes the best aperitif; alternatively, a dry sherry. Cocktails, while stimulating, are inclined to overwhelm the taste buds and spoil the delights of the dinner to come. A chilled dry sherry or Madeira served with a warming winter soup can't be bettered, though a light white wine suits a cream or cold soup.

Classic combinations of ice-cold vodka with caviar, a rosé with bouillabaisse and a sweet Sauternes with foie gras should be observed. Dry white wines are fine to imbibe with terrines and pâtés and a muscadet goes down excellently with seafood.

Sauces should also play a part in the selection of wine: cream or cheese-based sauces are complemented by dry to medium-dry fruity whites; those with tomato or spicy bases suit a dry red wine or fuller bodied white. Fruit garnishes and curries or oriental-style dishes deserve slightly sweeter wines.

Egg dishes and smoked or salted fish present a problem as they really do not marry well with any style of wine, though some people do enjoy either Champagne or a Beaujolais with eggs. Probably the best accompaniment for smoked salmon or eel is aquavit or vodka, alternatively, try a very dry sherry.

As a fitting complement to the food served, it is important that the wines be carefully selected. Nothing can upset a finely tuned palate more than a poor quality wine or one with too sharp or overpowering a flavor.

Although rules have relaxed to the point where some say anything goes, there are certain conventions which have evolved over the years and are worth noting because they have been tested and proved right again and again. White

wine does taste better than red wine with fish; red tastes better than white with cheese. Chilled rosé or light red wines suit the mood of outdoor summer lunches; sweet wines, such as Sauternes, taste best with sweet foods.

The rules to consider for styles of wines: choose richer wines in winter, lighter wines in summer. Serve dry wines before sweet; young wines before older wines, white before red, light-bodied before those with fuller flavor, chilled

Avoid serving wine with salads that are tossed in vinaigrette dressing, although a very acidic white might be acceptable. If serving pasta, any red wine is in order, even a good quaffing one.

A choice of dry red table wines should be offered with the main course and the cheese plate. Poultry, such as duck or turkey, can take the lighter reds, game birds the heavier-bodied reds. Goose, which is oilier, will need a red wine with more acid. The exception to the red wine with cheese rule is blue vein cheeses, which are more suited to a Sauternes-style sweet wine.

Desserts naturally call for sweet wines such as a spätlese-style, Frontignan or Champagne. A soft, rich pudding is a very good reason for uncorking a great Sauternes. Old-fashioned puddings such as bread and butter, now back in favor but lighter in the translation, gain new sophistication when accompanied by a not too dry Riesling. Fresh fruit or fruit-based desserts need a Sauternes. Champagne is not a happy partner for acidic or citrus fruit or chocolate.

If a liquor or liqueur is used in the dessert recipe, by all means serve it as an accompaniment. Ice cream and sorbet are best served alone. With coffee, offer dessert wines such as port, tokay, a liqueur muscat or aged brandy.

Remember that the temperature of wine at the time of serving is also important: white wines are better cold, red wines at room temperature. Cold, however, does not mean frozen; if the wine is too cold, appreciation is impossible. Not ignoring the delights of a chilled Beaujolais, generally red wines should be brought gradually to room temperature before serving.

As some very old red wines throw a crust in the bottle, it is best to decant them to prevent pouring the sediment into the wine glasses.

Finally, a pitcher of iced water should always be available at the table so that water can be used as a palate cleanser between different wines.

Left: Many vintage red wines should be decanted well before serving, otherwise any sediment from the bottle may be poured into the glass
Below: Pretty china, sparkling glassware and a mass of garden flowers sets the scene for successful entertaining

SETTING THE SCENE

The pleasures of the table do not lie with the food and drink alone. Presentation is a vital ingredient in successful entertaining. A beautifully set table with fine china, silverware and crystal glasses is always pleasing. Add to this the delicate perfume of fresh flowers (nothing that will overpower the food), the warm glow of candles, imaginative touches such as place-cards, individual salt and pepper or pots of butter, and the atmosphere is ripe for a superb evening.

Beautiful china and glassware do justice to your efforts in the kitchen and, in the long run, you'll be rewarded for choosing a limited number of good things rather than an assemblage of tableware that's second best.

If your lifestyle and storage space calls for only one set of good china, we suggest you choose white. Not only does white best enhance food of any kind, but it co-ordinates with everything else – linen, table accessories, ovenware, serving dishes – and it is a basis on which to build other pieces. Contrasting entrée or dessert plates in pastels, brights or patterns can lift a basic all-white setting.

You should also look for quality in glassware. Experts say that glasses should always be transparent, colourless and crystal-clear to allow wine to show its true color. (The only acceptable colored glass is in tumblers for punch or juices.)

All chilled wine should be served in stemmed glasses and the glass held by the stem. Do not cup the glass in the hand or the contents will lose their chill rapidly. Red wines and Cognac served at room temperature may be cupped and warmed by the palms of the hands, but never artificially.

The fundamental shape is the goblet or claret glass, a perfectly acceptable shape for any kind of wine, even, at a pinch, a grand Champagne. The shape, size, pattern and length of stem will vary. Choose the longer stem for white, the larger bowl for red. The ideal Champagne glass is tall, stemmed and a flute or tulip shape.

Never be tempted to buy wide, flat Champagne glasses or saucers which allow the bubbles to dissipate too quickly.

Table wine glasses should hold between 5 fl oz and 8 fl oz and should never be filled to the brim. A little space should be left for the bouquet to collect, and most glasses have a slight narrowing towards the lip to concentrate this bouquet. Refill glasses before they have been emptied entirely.

Sherry glasses should hold about 2 fl oz; port glasses a little less. To be true to its origins, a fine French dessert Cognac should be served in a small,

tulip-shaped glass, almost a tasting glass; the brandy balloon is an English invention and virtually unknown to the French.

Chilling Champagne flutes or white wine glasses in the freezer is a thoughtful touch, while warmed brandy glasses always elicit appreciative comments.

When you are serving a number of different wines, make sure you have fresh glasses for each, even if it means quickly washing and drying them and returning them to the table. Good wine deserves to be savored, untempered by the taste or scent of anything else.

A canteen of good silver flatware is a worthwhile investment, though these days it is not really necessary to include fish knives and forks and fruit knives and forks. For entertaining outdoors, a good set of knives and forks with serrated edges is handy.

When eating alfresco, set the scene just as carefully and imaginatively as if it were the dining room of your house. Remember that breezes can blow and even the lightest zephyr can send everything flying – a good reason for eschewing paper plates and napkins. An inexpensive bolt of colorful cotton can yield a stack of handy napkins for outdoor use. If you don't wish to carry your china outside and opt for plastic table-

ware, make sure that it is of good quality, strong and durable.

Inside or out, the colors you choose for your cloth, napkins, the flowers, the lighting will determine the mood: quiet and intimate, warm and cosy, bright and colourful, flowery and feminine or sleek and sophisticated. Or choose a theme for your entertaining: Japanese, Italian, black and white (with food to match). The only limit is your imagination.

A veritable treasure trove of table-cloths is useful for ringing the changes. Our *Vogue* editors suggest using some of the more strikingly patterned sheets. Ribbons are one of the decorating ploys that add instant charm to any table: to tie around napkins in matching and contrasting colors; trailing from the centerpiece to the hem of the cloth at each placesetting.

Keep a cache of tiny flowering plants in small pots to be wrapped in muslin and tied with a pink bow, or placed in stiff brown paper bags tied with straw for a country mood.

Colors can take their cue from the season: in summer, a green and white theme, warming browns and russet tones in winter; or from the centerpiece, perhaps a prized antique mug painted in mauves and pinks. Pattern on pattern, if used confidently, can make a statement:

a flowered chintz tablecloth is a more dramatic backdrop for flowered china than the traditional white damask.

Always keep an eye open for the unexpected in your tablesettings; idiosyncratic touches add whimsy; a collection of shells for the center-piece, small glass birds sitting on each napkin, or sea salt and cracked peppercorns piled in individual scallop shells at each placesetting.

For more formal occasions, consider the additions of hand written menus on color coordinated paper, the music of Mozart or Tchaikovsky playing softly in the background, a single white flower in a tiny vase at each placesetting.

Rather like organizing a wardrobe, setting the scene is a matter of building up layers. Try to paint a picture: the room, the table, the food. Color, balance and texture are all important.

Far left: A simple arrangement of pebbles and rockery plants adds an unusual centerpiece for this alfresco setting
Left: A mass of candles, ponsiettas, and co-ordinated colors create maximum festive feel with minimum effort
Above: Whether eating outside or in your home, the colors, cloth, tableware and centerpiece you choose will determine the mood of the evening

ALFRESCO INFORMALITY

Southern California's uniformly pleasant weather and abundance of fresh fruits, vegetables and seafood has led to an informal life style centered around the outdoors. While other parts of the United States may not be as fortunate year-round, summer brings California's lifestyle to all parts of the country.

Given the prospect of a sunny day, Americans lay claim to the outdoors as a second dining room. The terrace, the garden, the boat, the pool and the pier are perfect places for entertaining and savoring foods of all kinds: fresh shellfish, crisp tips of asparagus, voluptuous fruit ripened by the sun.

We freely borrow culinary ideas from cultures other than our own, modify and refine them to suit ourselves and the informality of our way of life. We've come a long way since outdoor eating meant a limp sandwich and a giant steak slapped on a grill.

SUMMER COUNTRY LUNCH
—————FOR SIX—————

Cherry Tomatoes Stuffed with Avocado
Cucumbers Stuffed with Herb Cheese

Fillet of Beef with Walnut Stuffing
Chicken Salad with Honeydew Melon and Ginger Mayonnaise
Snow Pea and Artichoke Salad
Green Salad

Hummingbird Cake

An alfresco lunch party is one step above a picnic. Gather portable furniture and a medley of cold dishes and set up position in the most idyllic spot that you can find. Lunch starts with easily managed and quickly prepared stuffed vegetables: cherry tomatoes filled with avocado, sour cream, lime and lemon juice and cucumbers filled with herb cheese.

Two delectable summer dishes follow: fillet of beef with orange and port-laced walnut stuffing plus a chicken and honeydew salad with a ginger mayonnaise. Snow pea and artichoke salad and a vinaigrette-dressed salad are crisp accompaniments.

After such a light meal, there is a place for a rich dessert. Hummingbird cake, flavored with chopped bananas and crushed pineapple and sandwiched together with pieces of mango and cream cheese frosting, is a luscious and suitably tropical finale.

Left: Setting the scene for a summer country lunch

CHERRY TOMATOES STUFFED WITH AVOCADO

2 punnets cherry tomatoes
salt
freshly ground pepper
sugar to taste
2 ripe avocados
2 tablespoons sour cream
4 teaspoons lime juice
4 teaspoons lemon juice
3 tablespoons finely chopped mixed parsley and chives
Tabasco sauce
sprigs of parsley to garnish

Cut thin slices from the tops of the tomatoes, remove the seeds and pulp (a small melon ball scooper is good for this).

Sprinkle with salt, pepper and sugar, invert on paper towels and leave the tomatoes to drain.

Mash the avocados and combine with the remaining ingredients. Season with Tabasco and black pepper to taste. Fill the tomatoes. Serve chilled, topped with sprigs of parsley.

CUCUMBERS STUFFED WITH HERB CHEESE

You can vary this recipe depending upon the herbs you have growing in the garden. Make the cheese filling a day in advance; this allows the herb flavors time to develop.

Peel and halve the baby cucumbers

and remove the seeds. If baby cucumbers are not available, use large cucumbers and cut them into 1-inch lengths.

Place the fresh herbs in a food processor and chop finely, add softened cream cheese and combine well. Alternatively chop the herbs finely by hand and beat into the softened cheese. We suggest you use garlic, parsley, fresh basil, a little tarragon, and lots of chives and black pepper. Green peppercorns and chopped mint are another good combination. Allow the mixture to stand overnight before piling into the cucumber shells. Sprinkle with green peppercorns and serve garnished with nasturtium leaves.

Above: Cherry tomatoes stuffed with avocado; Cucumber stuffed with herb cheese

FILLET OF BEEF WITH WALNUT STUFFING

walnut stuffing:

2 tablespoons butter
$\frac{1}{4}$ cup finely chopped onion
$\frac{1}{4}$ cup walnuts, ground finely
1 egg, beaten
$\frac{1}{2}$ bunch parsley, chopped finely
1 teaspoon finely grated orange rind
2 tablespoons port

for the fillet:

fillet of beef, weighing about 1$\frac{1}{2}$ lb
French mustard
freshly ground pepper
butter for frying

To make the stuffing: melt the butter in a frying pan and cook the onions until soft. Remove the pan from the heat and add the walnuts, beaten egg, parsley, orange rind and port.

To prepare the fillet: cut any fat and sinew from the fillet with a sharp knife. Cut a slit lengthwise in the fillet.

Rub the inside and outside of the fillet with a little French mustard and season with black pepper. Fill with the stuffing and then tie the fillet with string to retain the shape.

Heat the butter in a heavy-bottomed frying pan and then brown the fillet on all sides. Transfer to a roasting pan and cook in a preheated 400° oven for 25 to 30 minutes. (The fillet will go on cooking after it is removed from the oven.) Allow to cool.

Serve cold, cut in generous slices.

Below: Fillet of beef with walnut stuffing; Snow peas and artichoke salad (page 24); Green salad (page 24)

CHICKEN SALAD WITH HONEYDEW MELON AND GINGER MAYONNAISE

6 chicken cutlets
1 cup white wine
1 cup water
1 teaspoon black peppercorns
celery tops
2 stalks celery, chopped finely
4 tablespoons finely chopped parsley
¼ large honeydew melon
ginger mayonnaise:
⅔ cup good-quality mayonnaise
⅔ cup sour cream
grated rind of 1 small lemon
4 tablespoons lemon juice
2 teaspoons honey
piece of gingerroot about 3 inches long, peeled
    and grated
salt
freshly ground pepper

Place the chicken, wine and water in a saucepan, adding more water if necessary. Add the peppercorns and celery tops for flavor. Bring to the boil, and poach gently until the chicken is cooked.

When cooked, remove the chicken from the stock. Cut the chicken diagonally into bite-sized pieces. Place the chicken in a bowl with the celery and parsley. Peel the melon and cut into pieces. Add to the chicken mixture.

To make the ginger mayonnaise: blend the mayonnaise, sour cream, lemon rind, lemon juice and honey. Add the ginger to taste. Season with salt and pepper.

Dress the salad with the mayonnaise and serve at room temperature.

SNOW PEAS AND ARTICHOKE SALAD

Lightly steam some trimmed snow peas and allow to cool. Combine with fresh or canned artichoke hearts and a little freshly chopped tarragon. (If using fresh artichoke hearts, it will be necessary to sprinkle them with a little fresh lemon juice.) Toss the salad in a well-seasoned vinaigrette before serving.

GREEN SALAD

Use a selection of salad greens; we suggest Bibb lettuce, alfalfa sprouts, mung bean sprouts, celery leaves and chopped chives. Toss in a well-seasoned vinaigrette before serving.

Above: Chicken salad with honeydew ginger mayonnaise

HUMMINGBIRD CAKE

cake mixture:
2½ cups all-purpose flour
2¼ cups sugar
1 teaspoon salt
1 teaspoon baking soda
1 teaspoon ground cinnamon or garam masala
3 eggs, beaten
1½ cups oil
1½ teaspoons vanilla
1 8-oz can crushed pineapple, undrained
2 cups chopped bananas (the riper the better)
cream cheese frosting:
½ cup butter
1 8-oz package cream cheese
1 teaspoon vanilla
3¾ cups (1 lb) powdered sugar
a little milk if necessary
some pieces of mango to taste
fresh flowers to decorate

To make the cake: combine the dry ingredients in a large mixing bowl. Add the eggs and the oil, stirring well until the dry ingredients are moistened. Do not beat. Stir in the vanilla, crushed pineapple and bananas.

Spoon the batter into 3 well-greased, and floured 8-inch cake pans. Bake in a preheated 350° oven for 25 to 30 minutes or until the cakes are cooked; a skewer inserted in the cakes will come out clean. Cool in the pans for 10 minutes before turning out on to a wire cooling rack.

To make the frosting: beat together the butter, cream cheese and vanilla. Gradually beat in the powdered sugar, adding a little milk if necessary. (Alternatively process the butter, cream cheese and vanilla in a food processor. Add the powdered sugar and process again.)

Divide the frosting between two bowls. Add the mango to the frosting in one bowl and use to spread between the layers of the cake. When the cake is assembled, spread the frosting in the second bowl over the top and side of the cake. Decorate with fresh flowers and serve.

Right: Hummingbird cake

24

Fresh Tomato Pasta with Ham, Cream and Mushroom Sauce

Chicken Breasts Stuffed with Shrimps and Baked in Pastry
Salad of Romaine, Avocado and Quail Eggs

Mango and Macadamia Nut Ice Cream with Kiwifruit Coulis
Melting Moments

POOLSIDE GATHERING
—FOR SIX—

swimming pool is a delightful focal point for relaxed summer lunch parties. Set up the table by the water's edge, with informality as the keynote. This lunch has been designed for the cook who likes to prepare the dishes in advance so that all attention can be lavished upon the guests once they arrive. The dessert can be prepared the day before, the balance of the food should be made in the morning to insure that it looks absolutely fresh when it arrives on the table. The courses are purposely very different, but all have appealing color and texture. Most importantly, they can be carried with ease from kitchen to poolside.

Fresh tomato pasta, bought at specialist shops, is the basis of a pretty first course. A rich ham, cream and mushroom sauce is piled in the center of the pasta strands. Chicken breasts stuffed with shrimps make a delicious main course, the light crispy pastry blending well with the spicy filling.

A salad of romaine, cherry tomatoes, avocado and quail eggs balances the menu from the health point of view (remember the importance of eating your greens!).

Mango and macadamia nut ice cream is served with a sauce of kiwi-fruit and Kirsch, plus melting moments cookies. The combination of crunchy cookie and creamy smoothness provides the basis of many a successful dessert.

FRESH TOMATO PASTA WITH
HAM, CREAM AND MUSHROOM SAUCE

¾ lb fresh or packaged tomato noodles
butter
sauce:
4 tablespoons butter
¼ lb button mushrooms, sliced
4 slices ham, chopped
1 clove garlic, crushed
chopped fresh basil to taste
salt
freshly ground pepper
1¼ cups cream
to serve:
freshly grated Parmesan cheese
chopped fresh parsley

Cook the noodles in boiling, salted water for 2 minutes if using fresh pasta, 15 minutes if using dried. Drain, return the noodles to the saucepan and stir in sufficient butter to coat the pasta well.
To make the sauce: sauté the mushrooms lightly in butter. Add the chopped ham, garlic, basil, salt and pepper. Stir in the cream and heat through. Pour the sauce over the noodles, sprinkle with cheese and chopped parsley and serve.

Left and Far Left: Fresh tomato pasta with ham, cream and mushroom sauce

CHICKEN BREASTS STUFFED WITH PRAWNS AND BAKED IN PASTRY

½ cup butter
½ bunch green onions, chopped
1 clove garlic, crushed
1 lb raw shrimps, peeled and deveined,
  chopped roughly
2 tablespoons brandy
1 tablespoon flour
2 tablespoons dry vermouth
½ cup cream
6 boneless chicken breasts
salt
freshly ground pepper
extra flour to dust chicken
12 sheets phyllo pastry (about 12 oz)
melted butter
beaten egg to glaze
to garnish:
cooked shrimps
fresh dill

Melt half the butter, add the green onions and garlic and sweat gently for 1 minute. Add the shrimps and cook for 30 seconds. Pour in the brandy and flame.

Mix the flour, vermouth and cream together and stir into the shrimp mixture to thicken it. Season and cool.

Flatten each chicken breast slightly with the side of a mallet. Divide the mixture among the chicken breasts and fold each one over. Season each breast with salt and pepper and dust with flour. Fry carefully in the rest of the butter until the chicken is three-quarters cooked.

Brush 2 sheets of pastry with melted butter and wrap one chicken breast in the pastry like a parcel. Glaze with beaten egg. Place on a buttered baking sheet. Wrap remaining breasts in the same way. Cook in a preheated 350° oven for 15 minutes. Serve garnished with shrimps and sprigs of dill.

SALAD OF ROMAINE, AVOCADO AND QUAIL EGGS

1 head of romaine
1 large avocado
12 quail eggs boiled for 2 minutes, shelled
  and quartered
10 snow peas, blanched
½ sweet green pepper, cut in julienne
  (matchstick) strips
½ sweet red pepper, cut in julienne
  (matchstick) strips
¼ lb black grapes
12 cherry tomatoes
alfalfa sprouts for garnish
dressing:
1 teaspoon walnut oil
4 tablespoons safflower oil
1 tablespoon white wine vinegar
salt
freshly ground pepper

Arrange the lettuce leaves on a flat dish and fill each leaf with sliced avocado and quail eggs. Garnish with snow peas, green and red peppers, grapes and tomatoes.
To make the dressing: put all the ingredients in a jar, close the lid and shake well. Pour the dressing over the salad and top with the alfalfa sprouts.

Above: Chicken breasts stuffed with shrimps and baked in pastry
Left: Salad of romaine, avocado and quail eggs
Right: Mango and macadamia nut ice cream with kiwifruit coulis

28

MANGO AND MACADAMIA NUT ICE CREAM WITH KIWIFRUIT COULIS

$1\frac{1}{2}$ quarts vanilla ice cream
1 cup unsalted macadamia nuts, chopped
  roughly

mango ice cream:
3 ripe mangoes or 2 cups canned mango purée
2 tablespoons sugar or to taste
$\frac{2}{3}$ cup water
2 teaspoons lemon juice
1 tablespoon chopped preserved ginger
$1\frac{1}{4}$ cups cream
pinch salt

kiwifruit coulis:
4 kiwifruit, peeled and chopped roughly
Kirsch to taste
sugar to taste

to serve:
chopped macadamia nuts
sliced kiwifruit

Soften the vanilla ice cream for about 10 minutes in the refrigerator. Place it in a large bowl and beat in the nuts. Spoon the mixture into a wet 6-cup mold, working well up the side and leaving a hollow in the center for the mango ice cream. Cover and freeze for 30 minutes. *To make the mango ice cream:* purée the fresh mangoes, if using, to give 2 cups. Strain the purée. Boil the sugar and water together for 10 minutes then allow to cool. Add the mango, lemon juice and ginger. Spoon into a container, cover and freeze until hard around the edge. Transfer to a bowl and beat.

Whip the cream and salt until stiff and fold into the frozen mango mixture. Return to the freezer until the ice cream is almost firm. Beat again, then spoon into the middle of the ice cream mold. Cover and freeze until ready to serve.
To make the kiwifruit coulis: purée the chopped kiwifruit. Add the Kirsch and sugar to taste. Strain the coulis if desired. *To serve:* unmold the ice cream on to a serving platter. Decorate with chopped macadamia nuts and kiwifruit slices. Serve with the coulis. Pass the melting moments around separately.

MELTING MOMENTS

1 cup butter
$\frac{1}{3}$ cup powdered sugar
$1\frac{1}{4}$ cups all-purpose flour
scant $\frac{1}{2}$ cup cornstarch
vanilla to taste

Melt the butter in a saucepan, cool and beat in the powdered sugar. Fold in the sifted flour and cornstarch and add vanilla to taste. Spoon teaspoonfuls on to buttered baking sheets. Cook in a pre-heated 300° oven for 20 minutes. Cool a little on the baking sheet, then transfer to wire racks. Store in an airtight tin.

30

SUMMER LUNCH
—————FOR SIX—————

Prelunch Honey Cup

Sweetbread and Asparagus Tarts with Tomato Coulis

Sea Perch with Sorrel Sauce
Snow Peas

Fresh Fruit with Chaudeau Sauce
Rose Water Meringues

The inventive use of sauces is the easiest way to transform an ordinary dish into something special. Witness their impact in this creative menu for a sultry summer afternoon's eating. Conveniently, most sauces can be made beforehand, even the egg-based ones, so long as they are not reheated, only warmed. In summer a light aperitif is welcome as a thirst quencher before an outdoor meal. Guests can mingle informally, sipping long cool glasses of honey cup.

A lot of preparation time is required for the sweetbread and asparagus tarts and so the other courses have been deliberately kept simple. Sweetbreads are not everybody's favorite but their distinct flavor gets a fillip when teamed with asparagus and tomato coulis.

Green, yellow and white is the unusual color scheme of the main course with sorrel sauce the order of the day. Fillets of sea perch are baked with slices of avocado, grapefruit and mango for ten minutes, but definitely no longer as the avocado will become bitter. Crunchy snow peas complete the look and the flavor.

The dessert: fresh fruit doused in a rich sauce of Cointreau, egg yolk and white wine is served with crisp rose water meringues.

Left: The ideal spot for prelunch honey cup

PRELUNCH HONEY CUP

2 tablespoons honey
1 750-ml bottle dry white wine
2 lemons, sliced thinly
crushed ice
2½ cups lemonade or soda water
a sprig of mint

In a large pitcher, mix the honey with the wine. Add the lemons and leave in a cool place for about 2 hours.

When ready to serve, add crushed ice to the pitcher and stir in lemonade or soda water. Add mint and serve.

SWEETBREAD AND ASPARAGUS TARTS

whole wheat pastry:
¾ cup whole wheat flour
6 tablespoons cold butter, diced
3 teaspoons lemon juice
3 teaspoons iced water

filling:
½ lb sweetbreads
2 cups chicken stock
1 cup dry white wine
1 carrot, sliced roughly
1 celery stalk, sliced roughly
2 shallot tops, chopped
6 cracked peppercorns
a pinch of thyme
1 bay leaf
1 parsley stalk
1 tablespoon butter
1 clove garlic, crushed
2 shallots, sliced thinly

asparagus:
5 stalks asparagus
1 teaspoon sugar
1 teaspoon lemon juice

sauce:
½ teaspoon arrowroot
¼ cup cream
basil sprigs to garnish

To make the pastry: place the flour in a large bowl and rub in the butter until the mixture resembles bread crumbs. Add the lemon juice and enough iced water to make a firm dough. (Alternatively make the pastry in a food processor: work the flour and butter together until the mixture resembles bread crumbs. Then add the liquids and process until the pastry forms a ball.) Roll out the pastry on a lightly floured board and line 4 lightly oiled 3-inch tartlet pans. Prick well with a fork and refrigerate for about an hour.

Cook the tart shells on the center shelf of a preheated 375° oven for 12 to 15 minutes or until the tarts are brown and crisp. Cool on a wire rack.

To make the filling: soak the sweetbreads in lightly salted water for about an hour, then drain and place in a saucepan. Cover with chicken stock, wine, carrot, celery, shallot tops, peppercorns and herbs. Bring to the boil, then reduce the heat and poach gently for 10 minutes. Remove the sweetbreads from the stock with a slotted spoon and set aside to cool.

Boil the stock rapidly until reduced by half and then strain into a pitcher. Discard the residue in the strainer. Place the stock in the refrigerator and skim off any fat that sets on the surface.

When the sweetbreads are cold, cut them into very small pieces and pan fry gently in butter with garlic and sliced shallot for about 3 minutes. Remove pan from heat and set aside.

To cook the asparagus: trim the ends and lay the asparagus stalks in a frying pan. Cover with water and add sugar and lemon juice. Bring to the boil, lower the heat and simmer for 1 minute. Remove asparagus and refresh under cold water. Drain, cut into bite-sized pieces and set aside.

To make the sauce: pour the reserved reduced stock into a saucepan and reheat gently. In a cup, mix the arrowroot to a paste with the cream, add to the stock and cook for a few minutes until the stock boils and thickens. Taste for salt and pepper.

To assemble: place the pastry shells on a baking sheet and place 1 tablespoon of sauce in each. Divide the sweetbreads and asparagus pieces among the shells and bake in a preheated 375° oven for 7 minutes. Serve each tart on a heated plate with a sprig of basil and a little of the hot tomato coulis on the side.

TOMATO COULIS

6 tablespoons butter
1 onion, chopped finely
6 tomatoes, peeled, seeded and chopped
3 cloves garlic, crushed
1 tablespoon fresh basil or 1 teaspoon dried basil
salt
freshly ground pepper

Melt the butter in a frying pan and sauté the onion for a few minutes. Add the tomatoes, garlic and basil and cook the mixture rapidly until thick. Add salt and pepper to taste.

Above: Sweetbread and asparagus tarts with tomato coulis

SEA PERCH WITH SORREL SAUCE

6 tablespoons butter
6 fillets sea perch
salt
freshly ground pepper
6 slices grapefruit
6 slices avocado
6 slices mango
sorrel leaves for garnish
sorrel sauce:
2 shallots, chopped very finely
½ cup tarragon vinegar
⅔ cup butter
¾ cup cream
1 teaspoon arrowroot mixed with juice of ½
   lemon
¼ lb fresh sorrel, chopped finely
salt
freshly ground pepper

To cook the fish: melt the butter in an ovenproof dish and add the fish fillets in one layer. Season well. Top each fillet with grapefruit, avocado and mango slices. Bake uncovered in a pre-heated 400° oven for 10 minutes (no longer, or the avocado will become bitter).

To make the sorrel sauce: place the shallots and vinegar in a saucepan and reduce to 1 tablespoon. Add the butter and melt over low heat. Add the cream, stir and bring to the boil. Add the arrowroot and lemon juice and cook until thickened, stirring constantly. Just before serving, add the sorrel, salt and pepper.

To serve: arrange the sea perch and fruit on a serving dish and garnish with sorrel leaves. Place the sauce in the center of the dish and serve immediately.

SNOW PEAS

36 snow peas, trimmed
½ cup water
1 teaspoon sugar
1 tablespoon butter
1 tablespoon lemon juice

Place the snow peas in a saucepan with the water and sugar. Bring to the boil, drain and immediately refresh under cold water. Drain again and return snow peas to saucepan with butter and lemon juice. Reheat and serve immediately.

ROSE WATER MERINGUES

whites of 6 large eggs
2¼ cups (1 lb) superfine sugar
1½ teaspoons rose water
1½ teaspoons vinegar

Preheat oven to 200°. Brush baking sheets with oil and dredge with flour. Shake off excess.

Beat the egg whites in a large mixing bowl until they hold stiff peaks. Still beating, gradually add 2 tablespoons of sugar. Beat well. Add the remaining sugar, 2 tablespoons at a time, and continue beating until the mixture is shiny and holds stiff peaks. Lastly fold in the rose water and vinegar with a metal spoon. Pipe or spoon small amounts of the mixture on to the baking sheets.

Before placing the meringues in the oven, turn down heat to the lowest setting, preferably 150°. Cook the meringues for 2 hours. Remove the baking sheets and turn off oven. Loosen the meringues carefully and return to the oven for another 30 minutes. Cool on wire racks and store in airtight tins.

Note: These meringues can be made well in advance if stored in an airtight container.

FRESH FRUIT WITH CHAUDEAU SAUCE

1 pint strawberries, hulled
4 kiwifruit, peeled and sliced
1 cup gooseberries or seedless green grapes
3 tablespoons Cointreau
Chaudeau sauce:
1 tablespoon Cointreau
4 egg yolks
1 cup dry white wine
¼ cup sugar

To prepare the fruit: marinate the strawberries and kiwifruit in the Cointreau for at least 2 hours. Add the gooseberries or grapes at the last minute. Serve with Chaudeau sauce.

To make the Chaudeau sauce: in top of a double boiler combine all the ingredients and whisk until smooth. Place saucepan over simmering water and beat constantly until mixture triples in bulk and is foamy. Serve immediately.

Left: Sea perch with sorrel sauce

LUNCH ON BOARD
FOR EIGHT

Hard-boiled Eggs with Pesto

or

Egg Pâté with Caviar and Melba Toast

Fish Terrine with Herb Mayonnaise

Boiled Lobster with a Selection of Sauces

Grapefruit Salad

Spinach Salad

Creamy Onions

Brandied Cheese and Fruit

Apple and Pecan Nut Cake

Dishes that are to be served on board a launch must be simple to prepare in a confined space. Light summery food that makes the most of seafood is particularly applicable.

Everything in this menu can be prepared in a well-equipped galley, apart from the fish terrine which must be made ashore before departure. If you intend going out for the day or weekend only, the moist apple and pecan cake and the brandied cheese can be prepared ahead.

The meal is a sequence of tantalizing easy-to-digest dishes, starting with a miscellany of entrées, to be served buffet-style. Included are a soft, delicately striped fish terrine, served with a herb mayonnaise; hard-boiled eggs stuffed with pesto; white onions in a creamy sauce; and a simply constructed pâté of egg and caviar.

Fresh lobsters are the perfect centerpiece for such a stylish nautical lunch. The succulent flesh should not be swamped by too many additional flavors – a few delicate sauces and a palate-cleansing pink grapefruit salad are all that is needed.

As appetites always seem to run high at sea, the inclusion of a healthy fruit and nut cake and a platter of fruit and cheese makes good sense.

Left: Fish terrine (page 36)

HARD-BOILED EGGS WITH PESTO

Pesto sauce is available in Italian food stores and some supermarkets. It is a blend of pounded basil leaves, garlic, pine nuts, salt, grated Parmesan cheese and olive oil.

4 hard-boiled eggs, shelled
4 tablespoons pesto sauce
8 capers
fresh basil to garnish

Slice eggs in half lengthwise. Remove yolks carefully, keeping the egg white halves intact.

In a small bowl, mash all the egg yolks with the pesto. Fill the whites with the pesto mixture, piling it up. Place a caper and a sprig of basil in the center of each egg. Arrange the stuffed eggs on a platter and serve.

EGG PÂTÉ WITH CAVIAR

12 hard-boiled eggs, chopped roughly
4 green onions, chopped finely
about ½ cup butter, melted
salt
freshly ground pepper
1 3½-oz jar caviar
parsley to garnish
Melba toast

Place the eggs in a large bowl, add the onions and stir in enough melted butter to hold the mixture firmly together. Add salt and pepper to taste. Pack into a buttered mold, cover and refrigerate, overnight if possible.

Unmold and spread the top with caviar and garnish with parsley. Cut in slices and serve with Melba toast.
Variation: Use both red and black lumpfish roe to decorate the pâté in place of the more expensive caviar.

FISH TERRINE

1 lb sole or any firm-textured white fish, bones
    and skin removed
⅔ cup cream
salt
freshly ground pepper
grated nutmeg
1 lb scallops, cleaned
3 egg whites
½ lb spinach
½ cup unsalted butter
¼ lb raw shrimps, peeled and deveined
4 green onions, chopped finely
2 tablespoons chopped fresh herbs

Place the fish in the bowl of a blender or food processor and process until smooth and shiny. Add half the cream and season with salt, pepper and nutmeg. Process briefly and then transfer the mixture to a bowl.

Repeat the process with the scallops and the remaining cream and transfer the mixture to a second bowl. Beat the egg whites until they hold soft peaks. Fold half the egg whites into the fish mixture and half into the scallop mixture.

Wash and blanch the spinach leaves and drain well. Purée in a blender or food processor. Add 2 tablespoons of the scallop mixture and 2 tablespoons of the fish mixture and set aside.

Melt the butter in the frying pan and cook the shrimps until just colored and firm. Add the green onions and remove the pan from the heat. When the mixture is cool, add it and the herbs to the spinach mixture in the blender or food processor and process.

Oil a 9 × 5 inch loaf pan and spread the scallop mixture on the base. Cover with the spinach mixture and, lastly, the fish mixture. Cover with foil. Put the terrine in a baking dish partly filled with hot water and cook in a preheated 350° oven for 1 hour or until set. Cool and then chill overnight. Serve sliced with herb mayonnaise.

HERB MAYONNAISE

3 egg yolks
salt
freshly ground pepper
1 tablespoon Dijon mustard
1 to 2 tablespoons lemon juice
1¼ cups oil
4 tablespoons chopped mixed herbs (parsley and basil) and spinach

Place the egg yolks, 1 teaspoon salt, pepper, mustard and lemon juice in a blender or food processor and process to mix ingredients.

With the motor still running, add the oil slowly in a thin, steady stream. Add chopped herbs and spinach, taste for seasoning.

BOILED CRAYFISH

Kill the live lobsters by inserting a knife between the body and tail to sever the spinal cord. (This will ensure that the lobsters will not toughen when they are cooked.) Place the lobsters in a large kettle of boiling water, preferably sea water. If not using sea water, add salt until you achieve the same taste as sea water. Bring the water back to the boil and cook for 10 minutes; allow longer if the lobsters are quite large. Remove from the water and cool.

Halve the lobsters and remove the digestive tracts. Arrange the lobster halves on a bed of ice on a large glass platter and serve with a selection of flavored sauces or white vinegar.

POLLY'S CREAM SAUCE

1¼ cups heavy cream, whipped
few drops of Tabasco sauce
½ to ¾ cup mayonnaise
a little tomato sauce
squeeze of lemon juice
salt
freshly ground pepper
chopped parsley, mint or chives to taste
canteloupe pieces or grapes (optional)
red or green peppercorns to garnish

Mix together the cream, Tabasco, mayonnaise, tomato sauce, lemon juice, salt and pepper and herbs.

Add the canteloupe or grapes, if using. Transfer to a bowl and scatter the peppercorns on top.

GREEN SAUCE

1½ cups good quality mayonnaise
4 tablespoons grated onion
4 teaspoons curry powder
4 tablespoons finely chopped parsley
½ cup sour cream

In a blender or food processor, blend all the ingredients until they are smooth and creamy.

Place in a covered container and chill overnight before serving.

Far left above: Hard-boiled eggs with pesto
Far left below: Egg paté with caviar
Above: Green sauce; lemon mayonnaise (page 38); Polly's cream sauce
Left: Boiled lobsters

LEMON MAYONNAISE

3 egg yolks
⅓ cup lemon juice
salt
freshly ground pepper
dry mustard to taste
2 to 3 cups good-quality vegetable oil
1 tablespoon canned green peppercorns,
    drained

Put the egg yolks, lemon juice, salt, pepper and mustard in a food processor or blender and process well. With the motor running, gradually add the vegetable oil until you have a good thick mayonnaise. Stir in the green peppercorns with a fork and transfer to a serving bowl. Decorate with a slice of lemon and sprig or two of fresh dill.

SPINACH SALAD

6 tablespoons olive oil
2 tablespoons lemon juice
2 cloves garlic, crushed
coarsely grated rind of 1 lemon
1 lb spinach, trimmed
salt
freshly ground pepper
lemon juice to serve

Heat the oil and lemon juice in a large saucepan. Add the garlic and lemon rind then add the spinach and toss over moderate heat until spinach is hot and each leaf is thoroughly coated with the olive oil mixture.

Season with salt and pepper and arrange on a platter that has been sprinkled with lemon juice.

GRAPEFRUIT SALAD

2 large grapefruit, peeled and segmented
1 onion, sliced thinly
2 tablespoons finely chopped mint
dressing:
3 tablespoons fresh orange juice
½ teaspoon finely grated orange rind
2 tablespoons Cointreau
3 tablespoons vegetable oil
1 teaspoon vinegar
pinch of cinnamon
½ teaspoon peppercorns

To make the dressing: put all the dressing ingredients in a screw-top jar, shake well and leave for 24 hours.

Arrange the salad ingredients on a dish or in a bowl and pour the dressing over just before serving.

CREAMY ONIONS

16 small white onions
2½ cups light chicken stock
6 cloves
fresh parsley and dill to garnish
sauce:
1 tablespoon butter
1 tablespoon flour
2 tablespoons milk
some stock from onions (see instructions)
1¼ cups cream
sherry to taste
freshly ground pepper

Place the onions in a saucepan with the chicken stock and cloves. Bring the stock to the boil, then reduce the heat and simmer until the onions are just tender. Drain the onions, strain and reserve the stock.

To make the sauce: melt the butter in a small pan and stir in the flour. Cook a little, then whisk in the milk, reserved stock, cream, sherry and pepper to taste.

Stir well, bring to the boil and cook for a few minutes. Pour over the onions and garnish with parsley and dill. Serve hot as a vegetable or cold as a salad.

BRANDIED CHEESE

1 lb ricotta cheese
6 tablespoons sugar
finely grated lemon rind to taste
2 tablespoons puréed brandied kumquats (see page 89) or apricot brandy
1¼ cups heavy cream
grated orange rind to decorate

Place the cheese in a bowl with the sugar and beat until smooth. Add the lemon rind and puréed kumquats or apricot brandy.

Whip the cream and mix with the ricotta mixture. Place in a piece of muslin or cheesecloth and twist the cloth so that the cheese forms a ball. Place in a sieve and put the sieve over a bowl. Refrigerate for several hours to allow the cheese to drain. The cheese will become firm.

Turn out on to a decorative platter, sprinkle with orange rind and serve with fresh fruit or fruit salad. This is especially good served with figs and bananas.

APPLE AND PECAN NUT CAKE

2 cooking apples
1 cup sugar
1¼ cups all-purpose flour
1 teaspoon baking soda
1 teaspoon cinnamon
1 teaspoon allspice
½ teaspoon salt
1 cup roughly chopped pecan nuts
½ cup butter
1 egg
12 pecan nuts to decorate

Peel, core and cut the apples into chunks as for apple pie, place in a bowl and mix with the sugar. Set aside.

Sift the flour, soda, cinnamon, allspice and salt into a large mixing bowl and mix in the chopped nuts.

Melt the butter in a pan, let cool slightly, then beat in the egg. Add the apples. Lightly mix in the flour/nut mixture and fold the ingredients together.

Spoon the mixture into a greased 8-in ring loaf tin. Bake in a preheated 350° oven for 45 to 55 minutes.

Turn out on to a wire rack to cool. Top with nuts and serve plain or with whipped cream.

Far left: Grapefruit salad
Left: Apple and pecan nut cake

Seafood Casserole

Roast Veal and Kidney with Mustard Sauce
Mushrooms Sprinkled with Sautéed Bacon
Blanched Spinach

French-style Apple Tartelettes

Cheese with Walnut and Whole Wheat Breads

TERRACE LUNCH
—FOR SIX—

L unching on the terrace always seems so civilized – a far cry from the hurried nature of the average workday lunch. French in inspiration, this is an elegant, well-balanced menu, featuring a little fish, a little veal, a little fruit and a little cheese (which is served before the dessert). Helpings are modest, just enough to make the diners feel replete.

Seafood casserole simmers quickly in a paprika-spiked sauce. If all the ingredients are ready, it can be cooked after the guests have arrived. Serve the casserole in individual soup plates to allow easy consumption of the delicious juices.

This is followed by roast veal, which is served with sautéed mushrooms, diced bacon and spinach instead of the conventional baked vegetables – a lighter alternative. Ask the butcher to bone the loin of veal and then roll it up and tie it with two veal kidneys inside. A mustard and parsley sauce unites the flavors together. Next a ripe, soft cheese of your choice is served with walnut and whole wheat breads.

French-style apple tartelettes need to be prepared in advance. One hour's resting time is required for the pastry which, if desired, can be made several days ahead and kept in the refrigerator or frozen for longer storage. A creamy apple purée is sandwiched between the pastry and apple slices (which are spread in a spiral pattern).

Left: Seafood casserole

SEAFOOD CASSEROLE

½ lb tomatoes, fresh or canned
12 raw prawns
1 teaspoon olive oil
1 teaspoon butter
2 raw potatoes, diced
½ yellow onion, chopped
1 teaspoon sweet paprika
¾ cup white wine (Fumé Blanc)
⅓ lb smoked eel, cut in small pieces
1 cup fish stock or water
⅔ lb red snapper fillets, cut in small pieces
⅓ lb scallops
salt
freshly ground pepper
cayenne pepper
3 cloves garlic, crushed
1 tablespoon chopped chives or parsley

If using fresh tomatoes, place in boiling water for 10 seconds. Drain and peel, cut in half and remove the seeds. Dice the flesh and reserve. If using canned tomatoes, drain, remove seeds and chop.

Cook the prawns for 1 minute in boiling water. Peel the prawns and devein.

Heat the oil and butter in a saucepan and sauté potatoes for a few minutes. Add the onion, fry for 1 minute and sprinkle in the paprika. Add the white wine and cook over moderately high heat for 2 to 3 minutes until liquid is slightly reduced. Add the smoked eel, stock and tomatoes. Simmer for 5 minutes. Add the red snapper, scallops and prawns. Simmer gently for about 5 minutes, then season with salt, pepper and a little cayenne. Stir in the garlic.

Serve the seafood casserole in a soup tureen with chopped chives or parsley sprinkled on the top.

ROAST VEAL AND KIDNEY WITH MUSTARD SAUCE

Ask your butcher to bone a loin of veal, roll it up with two veal kidneys inside and tie it with string.

1 tablespoon oil
1 teaspoon butter
1 veal roast with 2 veal kidneys (total weight about 3 lb)
salt
freshly ground pepper
1 carrot, diced
1 onion, diced
mustard sauce:
¾ cup dry white wine
1 cup water
2 tablespoons butter
1 tablespoon flour
2 tablespoons prepared hot mustard
2 tablespoons chopped parsley

Heat the oil and butter in a baking pan. Add the veal roll and brown on all sides. Sprinkle with salt and pepper and place in a preheated 425° oven. Roast for 10 minutes, then reduce oven temperature to 300°. Cook for a further 30 minutes, basting from time to time.

Add the carrot and onion to the baking pan and return to the oven for another 20 minutes or until the veal is cooked. Wrap the meat in foil and set aside in a warm place to rest while you make the sauce.

To make the sauce: remove the fat from the baking pan and discard. Pour in the wine and place the pan over high heat until liquid is reduced by half, scraping the base of the pan with a wooden spoon to incorporate juices that may have adhered to the pan. Add the water and bring the sauce back to the boil.

In a small bowl, mix the butter, flour and mustard. Add to the sauce, a little at a time, beating constantly with a whisk. When the sauce boils, it will thicken; strain it into a sauceboat. Stir in the parsley.

To serve: slice the veal on to a large platter and serve with mushrooms and sautéed bacon, and blanched spinach.

MUSHROOMS SPRINKLED WITH SAUTÉED BACON

Dice bacon and fry until crisp. Blanch small mushrooms in boiling salted water. Drain and keep warm. To serve, spoon the mushrooms around the veal roast and sprinkle with the bacon and a little chopped fresh parsley.

FRENCH-STYLE APPLE TARTELETTES

For a family dessert, make a large tart instead of the individual tartlets suggested here. Remember you will need about an hour's resting time for the pastry.

puff pastry:
1⅔ cups all-purpose flour
pinch salt
½ cup water
¾ cup plus one tablespoon hard butter, cut in slices about ½ inch thick
filling:
6 Granny Smith apples
2 tablespoons water
2 tablespoons cream
1 tablespoon sugar
powdered sugar for dusting tartelettes

To make the pastry: sift the flour and salt into a large mixing bowl and stir in enough water to make a firm dough. If pastry is too dry, add a little extra water. (Or process the flour and salt in a food processor, adding water through the feeder tube until the dough forms a ball.) Wrap the dough in a slightly damp cloth and refrigerate it for about 10 minutes.

Remove the dough from the refrigerator and roll out on a lightly floured board to a square about ½ inch thick. Place the slices of butter in the centre of the pastry and fold the four edges into the centre to envelop the butter completely.

Roll out to a rectangular strip ½ inch thick. You will now have a strip of pastry about twice as long as it is wide. Take the bottom end of the strip and fold it up to the middle of the strip. Fold the top third down to cover the first fold and to form a neat rectangle with no overlapping sides.

Turn the pastry a quarter turn to the right. Again roll pastry to a ½ inch thick strip and fold it as before. Make a small finger impression in the top right-hand corner of the pastry. Wrap the pastry in a slightly damp cloth and refrigerate for 20 minutes. This allows the butter and pastry to relax and combine at equal temperature.

Remove the pastry from the refrigerator and place it on the table so the finger mark is situated in the bottom right-hand corner. Repeat the rolling and folding of the dough four more times, resting the dough halfway through.

To make the tartelettes: peel the apples. Cut 2 of them in quarters and remove cores.

Above: Roast veal and kidney with mustard sauce

42

Cut each quarter in half again. Place the apple wedges in a saucepan with the water, cover and cook for about 5 minutes or until soft. Mash and cool.

Roll the puff pastry out on a lightly floured board until it is about $\frac{1}{8}$ inch thick and cut in circles to fit 6 tartelette molds. Line each mold with pastry and prick holes in the pastry with a fork to prevent shrinkage during cooking. Trim pastry edges with a sharp knife (cut cleanly, do not pull at the pastry). Place lined tartelette molds in refrigerator for 15 minutes.

Halve the remaining four apples, remove cores and cut into slices of about $\frac{1}{8}$ inch thick. Remove the molds from the refrigerator. Stir the cream into the apple purée and spread a layer of purée over the pastry. Starting at the outside,

place apple slices on top of the pastry moving in a spiral pattern towards the center. The apple slices should overlap each other so they leave no gaps.

Sprinkle sugar over the apples and cook in a preheated 450° oven for about 15 minutes. The tartelettes are cooked when the pastry is golden brown and crisp, and the edges of the apples are slightly browned. Sprinkle with powdered sugar and serve hot.

Note: The pastry may be used immediately or kept for a few days in the refrigerator. If you wish to keep it for longer, cut it into three pieces, wrap in plastic wrap and store in the freezer.

Right: French-style apple tartelettes
Below: Cheese with freshly bought walnut and whole wheat breads

43

Refreshing Tropical Cocktails

Guacamole with Corn Chips

Crayfish with Rice
or
Pineapple with Chicken Mayonnaise
Raw Vegetable Salad with Honey Dressing

Date Chocolate Torte

RIVERSIDE DINNER
FOR FOUR

There is a taste of the Caribbean in this meal which is designed for languorous consumption, perhaps on a boat moored upstream. West Indian style cocktails, laced with rum, fresh pineapple and coconut, are among the tropical flavorings used in a delightful and unexpected menu. The food is a blend of flavours and textures with fruit included in the cooked meat and fish dishes. The dishes can all be prepared the day before sailing and then stowed away on the boat.

Dining on a boat is a relaxed affair – and probably even more so after a rum punch, Ponche Crema or Bentley cocktail. During drinks, nibble on a palate-stimulating appetizer of corn chips and guacamole (this traditional avocado dip from Mexico has been eagerly embraced throughout the Caribbean region).

The raw vegetable salad is fruity too, with sliced banana and dried fruits, and this is followed by either pineapple with chicken or fresh crayfish with rice.

Date chocolate torte is deceptively simple to make but delicious to eat. Nuggets of chocolate, almonds and dates are bound together with a meringue mixture and the entire cake is then topped with cream.

BENTLEY

For a refreshing nonalcoholic drink, pour the freshly squeezed juice of ½ lemon into a tall glass, top with soda and add a dash of Angostura bitters. Add plenty of ice and serve garnished with lemon slices and cherries.

PONCHE CREMA
(Makes 2 litres)

3 eggs
grated rind of 1 lemon
1 14-oz can condensed milk
2 12-oz cans evaporated milk
1½ cups rum
Angostura bitters to taste

In a small bowl, beat the eggs with the lemon rind. Strain and add condensed and evaporated milks, rum and bitters to taste. Serve immediately in a pitcher or chill until required.

RUM PUNCH
(Makes 2½ litres)

If you want to experiment with your own combinations for a punch, remember that the proportions should be as follows: one part sour, two parts sweet, three parts strong and four parts weak.

1 cup lemon juice
2 cups sugar syrup
3 cups rum (preferably Barbados)
4 cups water, or 2 cups water and 2 cups
*   crushed ice*
Angostura bitters to taste

In a large pitcher, mix lemon juice, syrup and rum. Add water and ice, and bitters to taste. Serve immediately.

Left: Bentley, Ponche Crema and Rum Punch
Far Left: Guacamole with corn chips (page 46)

GUACAMOLE

This makes a very good dip for raw vegetables or corn chips.

2 large avocados, peeled and pitted
juice of 1 lemon
1 small clove garlic, crushed
Tabasco sauce to taste
a pinch of cumin
a pinch of salt
2 tomatoes, chopped finely
½ onion, chopped finely
chopped green chilies to taste (optional)
coriander leaves for garnish

In a bowl, mash the avocado flesh with the lemon juice, garlic, Tabasco and spices until it is a smooth paste. Carefully fold in tomatoes, onion and chilies.

Transfer to a serving bowl and garnish with fresh coriander leaves and serve with corn chips. Make guacamole the day it is served.

FRESH CRAYFISH WITH RICE

1 lb brown rice
½ lb pine-nuts, toasted
4 tablespoons chopped parsley
crayfish:
2 lb crayfish, peeled and heads removed
2½ cups cream
2 cups grated fresh or shredded coconut
freshly ground pepper
toasted coconut to garnish

To cook the rice: bring a large pot of salted water to the boil. Add the rice and stir well. Simmer for 30 to 40 minutes until the rice is cooked. Drain well and toss with the pine-nuts and parsley.
To cook the crayfish: simmer for 10 to 15 minutes in a mixture of the cream, coconut and pepper to taste.
To serve: spoon the mixture into the center of a serving platter and surround with rice. Sprinkle with toasted coconut.

PINEAPPLE WITH CHICKEN MAYONNAISE

This chicken mayonnaise is also very good with chopped ham and seedless green grapes.

3 cups water
1 tablespoon curry powder
2 bay leaves
1 teaspoon black peppercorns
4 chicken breasts, skinned
4 small ripe pineapples
toasted cashew nuts to garnish
dressing:
⅔ cup mayonnaise
⅓ cup sour cream
1 tablespoon fruit chutney
1 tablespoon lemon juice

Combine the water, curry powder, bay leaves and peppercorns in a large shallow saucepan. Bring to the boil, reduce the heat, add the chicken breasts and poach for about 12 minutes until the chicken is tender.

Cool the chicken in the stock, drain and shred the flesh. Mix with the mayonnaise, sour cream, chutney and lemon juice. Stir well.

Halve the pineapples lengthwise, including the green tops, and cut a thin slice from the bottom of each, so that they will stand steadily. Carefully remove the pineapple flesh, in one piece if possible; remove cores and slice thinly.

Place the chicken mixture in the pineapple shells. Place a pineapple shell on each plate, surrounded by pineapple slices, and garnish with a scattering of toasted cashew nuts.

Left: Crayfish with rice

RAW VEGETABLE SALAD WITH HONEY DRESSING

This is very much a mix and match salad. Vary the fresh fruits and vegetables with the season and try different combinations of nuts and dried fruit, such as a mixture of finely chopped carrots, cucumbers, celery, baby zucchini, red peppers, chives and apple, plus sliced banana and dates, cauliflower florets, sunflower seeds, alfalfa sprouts, almonds, cashews and sultanas, dried figs, apricots, peaches and pears.

To make the honey dressing: mix together equal quantities of fresh lemon juice, olive oil and honey in a bottle, cap and shake vigorously. Pour over the salad just before serving and toss well to distribute the dressing evenly.

DATE CHOCOLATE TORTE

$\frac{1}{2}$ *lb unblanched almonds*
$\frac{1}{2}$ *lb semisweet chocolate*
6 egg whites
$\frac{1}{2}$ *cup sugar*
$\frac{1}{2}$ *lb dates, chopped finely*
to decorate:
whipped cream
grated chocolate
nuts or strawberries

Place the almonds and chocolate in a blender or food processor and chop into chunky pieces. In a large bowl, beat the egg whites to stiff peaks and gradually add the sugar. Fold in the almonds, chocolate and dates. Pour into a greased, foil-lined 9-inch springform pan and cook in a preheated 350° oven for 45 minutes. Open the oven door slightly and allow the torte to cool in the pan. When cold, turn on to a platter and refrigerate overnight.

To serve: spread the top of the torte with whipped cream and decorate with grated chocolate, nuts or strawberries.

Note: This cake will crumble if cut while still warm. It will keep in the refrigerator for several days.

Above: Raw vegetable salad with honey dressing
Left: Date chocolate torte

Sunday Lunch Italian Style

——FOR SIX OR EIGHT——

Rotolo di Spinaci

Zuppa di Pesce della Mama Toti with Aïoli

Pizza-Pizza

Cestini con Mascarpone

Sunday affords time to linger over the lunch table. Good food and good company are the ingredients of an indulgent afternoon. Sometimes it is fun to keep the menu to a theme, such as Italian food. This lunch is one to be savored slowly. As is typical with Italian food, there is an emphasis on hearty flavoring.

The culinary adventure begins with rotolo di spinaci, a roulade-style dish made by rolling a filling of spinach and cheese (a versatile and ever-successful combination) inside a sheet of homemade pasta. This roll is steamed and then browned under a broiler at the last moment. Serve with thick tomato sauce for added impact.

The fish soup also needs careful attention just before serving, as browned fish pieces have to be added to the boiling fish stock and then cooked carefully to avoid disintegration. A spoonful of aïoli, the traditional garlic mayonnaise of the Mediterranean region, is the ideal accompaniment and flavor enhancer.

Although now as international as hamburgers, pizza should not be dismissed as "ordinary". A good homemade pizza will be savored because of the contrast of yeast-based crust and tasty toppings. For novelty, or fussy eaters, arrange the garnishes in stripes so that everybody can get the sort of topping he or she likes.

Such a substantial meal needs a light palate-cleansing dessert. The delicate cestini biscuits, which are shaped into baskets, can be made beforehand and then stored in an airtight container. When filled with mascarpone, a dash of Cognac and a little fresh fruit they form a perfect foil to the strong flavors that have gone before.

Left: Setting the scene for Sunday lunch Italian style

ROTOLO DI SPINACI
(Pasta Roll with Spinach)

stuffing:
2 lb fresh spinach
1 shallot, sliced finely
butter
1½ cups ricotta cheese
1 egg
salt
freshly ground pepper
nutmeg
½ cup grated Parmesan cheese

pasta:
2¼ cups all-purpose flour
1 tablespoon salt
3 large eggs, beaten

to finish rotolo:
½ cup grated Parmesan cheese
7 or 8 fresh sage leaves, chopped
½ cup butter, melted

To make the stuffing: wash and chop the spinach finely and steam in a colander over boiling water for about 3 minutes. Squeeze out all moisture.

Sauté the sliced shallot in the butter until transparent. Mix together the ricotta, egg, salt, pepper, nutmeg and Parmesan cheese. Add the spinach and shallot and mix well.

To make the pasta: sift the flour and salt in a bowl, add the eggs and gradually incorporate the flour to form a dough. Knead together well. On a lightly floured surface, roll out the dough to form a square, thin sheet about ⅛ inch thick.

To assemble: spread the stuffing thickly and evenly on the sheet of pasta, leaving about 2 inch border all around. Roll the pasta into a large sausage. Seal both ends by pressing down the pasta and folding the ends slightly.

To cook: carefully   the roll on to a large piece of cheesecloth. Wrap the roll in it, tying both ends with string. Cook in boiling salted water for about 15 minutes (if you have a fish poacher, the rotolo will fit perfectly).

When the rotolo is cooked, remove from the water, untie the cheesecloth, remove and cut the rotolo in slices about 1 inch thick.

To finish the rotolo: arrange the slices on a buttered ovenproof dish and sprinkle with the Parmesan. Add the chopped sage leaves to the melted butter and pour over the pasta. Place under a preheated grill until the pasta is golden brown. Serve immediately.

Note: The rotolo can also be served with a tomato sauce (see page 60).

AÏOLI
(Garlic Mayonnaise)

2 egg yolks
1 tablespoon French mustard
juice of 1 or 2 lemons
salt
freshly ground pepper
2 cloves garlic, crushed
2 cups olive oil

Place the egg yolks, mustard, lemon juice, salt, pepper and garlic in a blender or food processor and process until well blended. With the motor still running, gradually add the olive oil in a steady stream until you have a good thick mayonnaise. Transfer to a serving bowl and pass around with the soup.

ZUPPA DI PESCE DELLA MAMA TOTI
(Mama Toti's Fish Soup)

3 or 4 varieties of white fish (e.g. tile fish, bass, red snapper), cleaned, boned and cut into large bite-size pieces

stock:
bones, heads and trimmings of the fish
1½ quarts water
2 wine glasses white wine
2 onions, peeled and chopped
2 stalks celery
2 bay leaves
2 sprigs thyme
10 peppercorns
a few parsley stems

soup:
6 ripe tomatoes, peeled and chopped coarsely
2 cloves garlic, crushed
1 tablespoon chopped parsley
fresh oregano, to taste
½ teaspoon saffron strands or powder
salt
4 tablespoons oil

garnish:
chopped parsley
coarsely grated lemon rind
aïoli (recipe follows)

To make the stock: place the fish bones, heads and trimmings in a large saucepan with the water and white wine. Bring to the boil and skim off any scum. Add the onions, celery, bay leaves, thyme, peppercorns and parsley. Cover and simmer for 30 minutes.

Strain through a fine strainer, pressing down on the fish and vegetables to extract all the juices and flavor.

To make the soup: return the stock to a clean saucepan. Add the tomatoes, garlic, parsley, oregano, saffron and salt; set aside. Heat the oil in a heavy-bottomed cast iron saucepan and quickly brown the fish pieces. Discard all the oil and add the stock. Bring to the boil and cook for 4 minutes (be careful not to cook for too long or the fish will disintegrate).

Serve the soup immediately, sprinkled with chopped parsley and lemon rind. Pass around the aïoli separately so that each guest can add a spoonful to their soup.

Above right: Rotolo di spinaci
Right: Zuppa di pesce della mama Toti

PIZZA-PIZZA

dough:
2 packages active dry yeast
2 cups lukewarm water
5 cups all-purpose flour
¼ cup olive oil
1 tablespoon salt
garnish options:
anchovies and capers
sliced tomatoes, basil and garlic
rosemary and olives
onion rings, fried in oil
to cook:
½ cup virgin olive oil
salt
freshly ground pepper

Dissolve the yeast in 1 cup lukewarm water with 3 tablespoons of the flour. Allow the mixture to "sponge" – it should become frothy.

Place the remaining flour on a large board and make a well in the center. Add the oil, salt and yeast mixture, and gradually add 1 cup lukewarm water. Mix the dough well with your hands and, if it looks too dry, add more water, a little at a time. Knead the dough until it is elastic and shiny. Cover the dough with a fine film of oil, place in a bowl and leave to stand in a warm place for 1 hour.

Punch down dough and knead for another 5 minutes to remove all air. Spread the dough on a large oiled baking sheet and arrange your choice of garnish on top.

To cook: sprinkle the olive oil and salt and pepper to taste over the pizza-pizza. Cook in a preheated 475° oven for about 30 minutes or until golden. The pizza may be eaten hot or cold.

Above: Pizza-pizza
Right: Cestini con Mascarpone

CESTINI CON MASCARPONE
(Biscuit Cases with Mascarpone Filling)

mascarpone filling:
½ cup sugar
½ cup Cognac
2 eggs yolks, beaten
1 lb mascarpone
cestini:
⅓ cup sugar
grated rind of 1 lemon
¼ cup butter
2 egg whites
5 tablespoons sifted all-purpose flour
a pinch of salt
to decorate:
fresh dates
strawberries

To make the mascarpone filling: place the sugar and Cognac in a heavy-bottomed pan and dissolve over a low heat. Pour slowly over the egg yolks, beating constantly and vigorously. The mixture should resemble a zabaglione; light and fluffy and pale yellow. Leave to cool a little. Gradually add the mascarpone.

To make the cestini: beat the sugar, lemon rind and butter until fluffy. Add the egg whites and mix well. Gradually fold in the sifted flour and pinch of salt.

On an oiled baking sheet, draw two circles of about 6 inches diameter with your finger. In the center of each circle place 1 heaping tablespoon of the cestini mixture and, with the back of a spoon, spread out the mixture evenly and very thinly to fill the circles. Cook the cestini circles in a preheated 425° oven for 5 minutes. Prepare two bowls, about 4 inches in diameter, by oiling them very lightly and have them ready for the cooked cestini.

Remove the baking sheet from the oven and place it on the open oven door or in a warm place so that the cookies do not cool and become crisp. Lift one cookie with a spatula and quickly but gently press it into a prepared bowl to give it a round, "cup" shape. It will become hard very quickly, so you must work fast. Repeat with the other cookie. As soon as the cookies are firm, remove from the bowls and cool on a wire rack.

Repeat this process with the remaining mixture and store the cestini in an airtight container until ready to serve.

To assemble: spoon mascarpone mixture into cestini shells and make a small well in the center of each. Pour a little Cognac into the wells and decorate with fruit.

Smoked Fresh Rainbow Trout in Pastry with Horseradish,
Dill and Caper Sauce
Lemon and Herb Barbecued Loin of Lamb
New Potatoes

Mixed Green Salad in Crouton Baskets

Maraschino Ice Cream Cake with Vanilla and Raspberry Sauces

BARBECUE IN STYLE
FOR EIGHT

Barbecued food has a piquant smoky flavor quite unlike the oven-baked sort. Today, many kitchens have indoor barbecues that allow this form of cooking with none of the inconvenience of preparing food outside. Of course, the dishes can still be served in the open air to make the most of clement weather.

Some of these dishes take a long time to prepare, but the results do not look as if they were hard work. On the plate, the food looks fresh and fun rather than ornate and labored. Fresh trout is smoked then filleted and wrapped in a neat parcel of phyllo pastry and served with a flavorsome horseradish, dill and caper sauce. Green salad is prettily arranged in a deep-fried crouton basket.

The loin of lamb is the barbecued special. Marinated in lemon and ginger and then barbecued to a browny crispness, this is a perfect dish for the indoor barbecue, but, of course, could be adapted for the outdoor variety.

As the lamb and trout entrées need last-minute finishing, a dessert that can be made well in advance is included. Calorie-laden but sumptuously delicious, maraschino ice cream cake is served with vanilla and raspberry sauces.

Left: Maraschino ice cream cake with vanilla and raspberry sauces (page 55)

SMOKED FRESH RAINBOW TROUT IN PASTRY

2 large fresh rainbow trout (each fish should serve 4)
salt
2 bunches fresh dill
1 1-lb package phyllo pastry
melted butter
horseradish, dill and caper sauce to serve (recipe follows)
sprigs of fresh dill to garnish

Rub the fish inside and out with salt. Smoke in a smoker for approximately 8 minutes. Allow to cool, then run a knife down the center of each fish and peel back and remove the skin. Carefully remove the fillets from the bones and cut each fillet in two. You will have four pieces of fish from each trout.

Brush 4 layers of phyllo pastry with melted butter and stack one piece on top of the other. (You can wrap 5 or 6 pieces of fish from this prepared phyllo.) Wrap a piece of fish in the pastry, insure that the fish is well covered, but do not use too much pastry. Fold in the edges of the pastry and place on a baking sheet, seam side down. Brush with melted butter.

Roll up the remaining pieces of fish in the same way. Brush them again with melted butter and bake in a preheated 450° oven for 7 to 9 minutes or until light brown.

To serve: spoon a little of the sauce on to individual warmed serving plates. Add a pastry-wrapped piece of fish to each plate and garnish each with a sprig of dill and a few extra capers.

Left: Smoked fresh rainbow trout in pastry

HORSERADISH, DILL AND CAPER SAUCE

2 tablespoons softened butter
2 egg yolks
1 cup cream
salt
freshly ground pepper
1 tablespoon prepared horseradish
3 teaspoons tiny French capers
2 to 3 tablespoons chopped fresh dill

Whisk together the softened butter, egg yolks and cream in a bowl over simmering water or in a double boiler. Continue whisking until the sauce thickens slightly, then add the salt and pepper, horseradish, capers and dill. Fold in with a spoon and serve with the smoked fresh rainbow trout in pastry.

Above: Lemon and herb barbecued loin of lamb

LEMON AND HERB BARBECUED LOIN OF LAMB

leaves from 2 sprigs of fresh thyme
leaves from 2 sprigs of fresh rosemary
grated rind of $\frac{1}{2}$ lemon
juice of 1 lemon
4 cloves garlic, crushed
4 generous slices of fresh ginger, chopped
2 or 3 tablespoons honey
salt
freshly ground pepper
4 tablespoons butter
2 loins of lamb, bones removed
3 tablespoons oil
garnish:
sprigs of fresh herbs
strips of lemon rind

Place the thyme, rosemary, lemon rind and juice, garlic, ginger, honey, salt and pepper in a food processor or blender and process to a purée. Reserve 1 tablespoon of this mixture. Add the butter and continue to blend. Reserve 2 tablespoons of this herbed butter mixture.

Generously spread the herbed butter inside the loins. Roll up the loins and stitch together, using unwaxed dental floss or fine twine and a large darning needle.

Add the oil to the reserved lemon herb mixture (without the butter). Score the loins and rub the mixture well into the meat. Place in a china dish and pour over any mixture not adhering to the meat. Cover with plastic wrap and place the meat in the refrigerator for at least 4 hours or overnight if possible. Turn the loins in the oil mixture occasionally.

Transfer the meat to a roasting pan and cook in the center of a preheated 450° oven for approximately 20 minutes. Transfer the meat to a hot grill or preheated broiler and cook, turning frequently, for a further 15 minutes until the meat is crisp and brown on the outside.

To serve: carve the loins of lamb into 1 inch slices and serve topped with the reserved herb butter mixture, sprigs of fresh herbs plus fine strips of lemon rind.

54

MIXED GREEN SALAD IN CROUTON BASKETS

1 unsliced white sandwich loaf, one day old
peeled and bruised garlic to taste
vegetable oil for frying
salad:
a selection of salad greens to include endive,
*   baby spinach leaves and romaine*
vinaigrette dressing
¼ lb prosciutto, cut into julienne (matchstick)
*   strips*
8 quail eggs, poached

To make the crouton baskets: with a sharp knife, remove the end crusts and slice through the loaf to give 8 slices. Remove all crusts and carefully cut out the bread from the middle section of each slice to form 8 square baskets. Rub the baskets with the bruised garlic and then deep-fry in hot oil, one basket at a time, until golden. Remove from the oil and drain thoroughly on kitchen paper towels. Allow to cool.
To make the salad: combine the well-washed and dried salad greens and toss well with a little vinaigrette. Place the salad in the baskets and arrange the prosciutto in a lattice pattern on top of each salad. Top each with a poached quail egg and serve at once.

MARASCHINO ICE CREAM CAKE

6 egg yolks
¼ cup Maraschino liqueur
3 tablespoons sugar
3 cups heavy cream
6 tablespoons powdered sugar, sifted
1½ teaspoons vanilla
2 cups almond macaroons, crushed finely
2 cups cookie or cake crumbs, crushed finely
1 to 2 tablespoons Maraschino liqueur
to decorate:
toasted almonds
whole strawberries

To make the cake: whisk the egg yolks with the ¼ cup liqueur and sugar until thick. Place the bowl over a pan of boiling water and continue to whisk the mixture until thick and creamy. (A trail will be left on the mixture when the whisk is lifted.) Continue to beat until cool over a bowl of ice. In a chilled bowl, beat the cream until it holds soft peaks. Add the powdered sugar and vanilla and continue beating until well mixed. Do not overbeat. Using a metal spoon, carefully fold the cream into the egg mixture. Chill in the freezer for 30 minutes.

Mix the macaroon and cake or cookie crumbs. Butter a 9-inch springform cake pan and pour in 1 cup of the crumbs. Pat down firmly and evenly with the back of a spoon.

Remove the cream mixture from the freezer and stir. Pour ¼ of the mixture over the crumbs and freeze for 15 minutes. Sprinkle 1 cup of the remaining crumbs over the filling and sprinkle with some liqueur. Return to the freezer for another 15 minutes. Add another quarter of the cream filling and continue layering the crumbs and filling until you finish with a layer of cream filling on top. Be sure to freeze the cake for 15 minutes after adding a layer. When complete, cover and freeze the cake for at least 4 hours or until thoroughly set.
To serve: remove the maraschino ice-cream cake from the freezer 15 minutes before serving and turn out on to a serving platter. Decorate with the almonds and strawberries. Pass the vanilla and raspberry sauces separately (recipes follow). (Pictured on page 52.)

VANILLA SAUCE

2 cups cream
2 eggs, beaten
2 egg yolks, beaten
½ cup sugar
1½ teaspoons vanilla

Combine the cream, eggs, egg yolks and sugar in a heavy-bottomed saucepan and heat over a low heat, stirring continuously with a wooden spoon until the mixture is thick enough to coat the back of the spoon. Remove from the heat, beat in the vanilla. Cool and chill.

RASPBERRY SAUCE

1½ pints raspberries
2 cups water
½ to 1 cup sugar according to taste

Place 1½ cups of raspberries in a saucepan with 2 cups of water and sugar to taste. Bring to the boil and boil, covered, for a few minutes. Be careful that the raspberries do not boil over. Remove the lid from the pan and continue to boil gently for 10 to 15 minutes, stirring occasionally.

Remove the pan from the heat and allow to cool. Transfer the mixture to a food processor or blender and process until smooth. Reserve some whole berries for decoration and stir in the remaining raspberries and chill.

Left: Mixed green salad in crouton baskets

THE LONG WEEKEND

The most luxurious aspect of the weekend is that time is elastic which means that eating patterns may be paced according to your own internal time clock instead of one that dictates the beat of your working life.

Discretionary time is precious and should therefore be spent in the company of comfortable people with whom you share a common bond: family, close friends and neighbors.

The best food for lazy days like these is the kind we associate with county hospitality. It's hearty and generous and there's always enough for an unexpected guest or two. It's unpretentious cooking that spans age groups and makes people feel at home: old-fashioned vegetables such as parsnips and squash; muffins and cakes, warm from the oven; fresh juices and good aromatic coffee.

For house guests and visitors from Europe it represents the kind of welcome that will be appreciated for the privilege it is: an invitation to be included as part of the family.

CASUAL BRUNCH
──FOR SIX──

Fruit Juice

Sue's Fruit Compote

Huevos Rancheros
Frijoles Refritos

Cinnamon Crumb Cake

Coffee

T his brunch menu is designed for sharing with the family or with weekend guests. It is a meal to be eaten leisurely, perhaps to revive a palate jaded after the party that was held the night before.

Fruit juice and coffee, of course, are always welcome. The fruit compote, prepared the day before, consists of fresh fruits which have been steeped in a syrup of sweet dessert wine and sugar. If you are feeling brave so early in the day, serve it with a bottle of Sauternes-style wine.

Mexican food spices up the brunch table. Huevos Rancheros (or ranch-style eggs) are fried eggs served on warmed tortillas with a hot tomato sauce poured over them. They are quick to prepare and, served with Frijoles Refritos (refried pinto or red kidney beans), make a well-balanced, if surprising, course. The beans are first cooked, then fried with onion and garlic and mashed into a smooth fairly heavy paste. Their bland flavor complements the intense spiciness of the tomato sauce; the heavy, almost dry consistency of the paste contrasts with the brittle texture of the tortillas.

Cinnamon cakes are also typical of Mexico where a bulky cinnamon crumb cake would be dipped into hot chocolate as it was eaten.

Left: Cinnamon crumb cake (page 61)

59

SUE'S FRUIT COMPOTE

1 bottle Sauternes or any sweet dessert wine
½ cup sugar
3 ripe yellow peaches, peeled and halved
3 ripe apricots, halved
4 figs, peeled and quartered
½ cup green grapes
½ cup black grapes
1 cup strawberries, hulled

Boil the wine and sugar until reduced to half the original quantity. Place the fruit in a glass bowl and carefully cover with the boiling syrup. Allow to cool and chill in the refrigerator for 4 or 5 hours.

HUEVOS RANCHEROS

Huevos rancheros (or ranch-style eggs) are simply fried eggs served on warmed tortillas with hot salsa de jitomate (tomato sauce) poured over them.
To prepare the tortillas: sprinkle them with cold water and place them one at a time in a heavy ungreased hot frying pan for 1 minute or until they curl and soften; flip them over and cook for another minute. Alternatively, wrap a bundle of tortillas, which have been dampened with cold water, tightly in foil, and place in a very slow oven for about ½ hour or until soft and fresh.

SALSA DE JITOMATE
(Tomato Sauce)

4 tablespoons oil
2 large onions, chopped finely
2 cloves garlic, crushed
4 large tomatoes, chopped
1 teaspoon sugar
4 small hot chilies – or to taste, it should be hot!
salt
freshly ground pepper
freshly chopped coriander

Heat the oil and fry the onion and garlic until limp, add all the other ingredients except the coriander and cook gently for about 15 minutes. Taste for seasoning. Add the coriander and cook for a minute or two longer. This sauce can be made ahead and reheated.

Right: Huevos rancheros with salsa de jitomate

FRIJOLES REFRITOS
(Refried Beans)

1 lb dried pinto or red kidney beans
2 onions, chopped finely
2 cloves garlic, chopped
1 bay leaf
2 or more small, hot chilies
3 tablespoons lard or salad oil
salt
freshly ground pepper
1 tomato, peeled, seeded and chopped
8 tablespoons lard or bacon fat

Wash the beans and soak overnight; drain. Place in a saucepan with enough cold water to cover. Add 1 chopped onion, 1 garlic clove, the bay leaf and the chilies. Cover, bring to the boil, reduce heat and simmer, adding more boiling water as it cooks away. When the beans begin to wrinkle, add 1 tablespoon of the lard or oil. Continue cooking until the beans are soft. Stir in enough salt to taste and simmer for another 30 minutes, but do not add any more water. There should not be a great deal of liquid when the beans are cooked.

Heat the remaining lard in a frying pan and sauté the remaining onion and garlic until limp. Add the tomato and cook for about 2 minutes. Remove from heat and add 3 tablespoons of beans with some of the liquid from the pot and mash until you have a smooth, heavy paste.

Continue to mash the beans, bit by bit, adding the lard or bacon fat little by little. Taste for seasoning and add salt, pepper and a little more chili, if necessary. Do not overseason as the beans should have a fairly bland flavor. The beans are ready when a heavy, almost dry paste has formed.

CINNAMON CRUMB CAKE

crumb mixture:
2½ cups all-purpose flour
1½ cups sugar
¼ teaspoon salt
¾ cup butter

cake mixture:
2½ teaspoons baking powder
2 eggs, beaten
1 cup milk

cinnamon topping:
2 teaspoons cinnamon
4 teaspoons brown sugar
¼ cup soft butter
1¼ cups all-purpose flour

1 cup crumb mixture (see method)
to decorate:
powdered sugar
cinnamon

Grease and flour a 10-inch square baking pan, 4 inches deep.
To make the crumb mixture: in a large mixing bowl, mix together the flour, sugar and salt. Rub in the butter until mixture resembles bread crumbs and set 1 cup of this mixture aside for the cinnamon topping.
To make the cake: add the baking powder,

eggs and milk to the remaining crumb mixture and beat well. Pour the cake mixture into the prepared pan and set aside.
To make the topping: add the cinnamon, brown sugar, soft butter and flour to the reserved crumb mixture. Mix with your fingers until the mixture is crumbly. Sprinkle evenly over the uncooked cake and bake in a preheated 375° oven for 45 to 50 minutes. Cool in the pan on a wire rack. When cold turn on to a serving plate and sprinkle with powdered sugar and cinnamon.

Above: Sue's fruit compote

61

COUNTRY LUNCH
—— FOR SIX ——

Fresh Tomato Soup
Herb Biscuits

Jugged Hare
Boiled New Potatoes
Mustard Fruits

Fruits en Gratin

Hearty fare is what's required for a lunch in the country. All that fresh air inevitably seems to make appetites expand. The lunch makes the most of country produce, such as super-fresh vegetables and wild hare (those unable to catch their own can use the fresh or frozen variety available from specialty stores).

The meal kicks off with tomato soup. Surely one of the most fortifying of soups, this is also easy to make. Its flavor is accentuated by the addition, before serving, of a dollop of fresh or sour cream and a scattering of fresh shredded basil.

Herb biscuits are an enticing alternative to bread. A few sprigs of parsley and some mixed herbs are added to a conventional biscuit recipe.

Preparing jugged hare requires a little forethought, but it is well worth the effort. Pieces of a well-hung and skinned hare are marinated in wine and herbs for twenty-four hours. This is a very rich dish – the blood and liver of the hare can be added towards the end of cooking. Boiled new potatoes and a condiment such as mustard fruits or red currant jelly supplement the flavorsome juices. Jugged hare can be prepared a day in advance as it improves with keeping.

Whatever seasonal fruits are available can be used in the warm baked fruits en gratin, for example, a combination of peaches, canteloupe, strawberries, raspberries and blueberries. The fruit is soaked in Grand Marnier and covered with a rich cream, the top is sprinkled with sugar and the whole warmed under the broiler.

Left: Tomatoes stewing for fresh tomato soup

FRESH TOMATO SOUP

4 lb ripe tomatoes
2–3 cloves garlic, peeled
½ cup water
½ cup olive or grape seed oil
2 tablespoons chopped fresh parsley
salt
freshly ground pepper
1 tablespoon chopped fresh basil (optional)
to serve:
fresh shredded basil
fresh or sour cream

Wash the tomatoes and place in a large saucepan with the garlic cloves, water, oil, parsley and pepper. Cover and cook very slowly until the tomatoes are soft and skins can be easily removed.

Remove the tomatoes with a slotted spoon and set aside. Strain the liquid and reserve. Push the tomatoes through a sieve and discard seeds and skins. Add the reserved liquid to the puréed tomatoes until the soup reaches the desired consistency. Add salt and pepper to taste.

Heat the soup and add the basil if using. Do not allow the soup to boil again or the basil will discolor. Serve in individual heated bowls, with a spoonful of fresh or sour cream swirled on each portion and the remaining basil sprinkled on top.

HERB BISCUITS

1½ cups all-purpose flour
2½ teaspoons baking powder
½ teaspoon salt
2 teaspoons dried mixed herbs
a few sprigs of fresh parsley, chopped
⅓ cup shortening
¾ cup milk

Sift flour, baking powder and salt into a bowl. Add the herbs, parsley and shortening, and rub mixture together with the fingertips until the mixture resembles fresh bread crumbs.

Mixing with a fork, add just enough milk to make a soft dough. Knead briefly on a lightly floured board until dough is smooth. Roll out until ¾ inch thick and cut in rounds with a biscuit cutter.

Place on a greased baking sheet and bake in the center of a preheated 450° oven for 10 to 12 minutes. Serve warm.

Above: Fresh tomato soup with herb biscuits
Right: Jugged hare

JUGGED HARE

Frozen (and occasionally fresh) skinned hare is available in specialty food stores.

1 large young hare, well hung and skinned
  (blood and liver reserved, optional)
5 tablespoons olive oil
1¼ cups Cognac
1 clove garlic
1 bouquet garni
fresh bread crumbs or beurre manié to thicken
  (optional)
marinade:
1 sprig each of rosemary, thyme, sage, savory
1 onion, chopped finely
2 carrots, chopped finely
1 clove garlic, peeled
7 juniper berries
1 teaspoon black peppercorns
2 bottles red wine

Cut the hare in pieces and place in a non-metallic dish with the combined marinade ingredients. Set in a cool place for 24 hours, turning meat in marinade from time to time. Next day, remove pieces of hare and wipe dry. Transfer the marinade to a saucepan, boil rapidly for a few minutes and reserve.

To cook the hare: heat the oil over high heat in a large, enameled, cast-iron casserole. Brown the hare portions on all sides, then add warmed Cognac and flambé. Add the warm marinade, garlic and bouquet garni.

Cover casserole and cook hare over low to moderate heat for about 1½ hours, when the hare should be done. Remove pieces to serving dish and keep warm. Strain the cooking liquid into a saucepan and boil until reduced by half.

If you wish to add the blood and liver, chop the liver finely and place it in a large saucepan with the blood and about 1 tablespoon of reduced cooking liquid to thin it a little. Heat mixture to just below simmering point. Off the heat, slowly add the remaining reduced cooking liquid, whisking constantly with a wire whisk until it thickens. If the sauce needs more thickening, add the bread crumbs. Do not boil the sauce once the blood has been added or it will curdle.

If you do not wish to add the blood and liver, the sauce can be served as it is or reduced or thickened with bread crumbs or a little beurre manié (flour blended with an equal amount of butter).

Serve with boiled new potatoes and mustard fruits or red currant jelly. This dish can be prepared a day in advance as it improves with keeping overnight.

Right: Fruits en gratin

FRUITS EN GRATIN

1 cup strawberries
4 white peaches, peeled and pitted
1 canteloupe or honeydew melon, peeled and
  seeded
1 cup raspberries
1 cup blueberries (or substitute other berries
  and fruits in season)
⅘ cup Grand Marnier
2½ tablespoons sugar
sauce:
6 egg yolks
1 tablespoon cold water
2 tablespoons cream
2 tablespoons sugar

To prepare the fruit: wash and hull the strawberries and, if very large, cut in half. Cut the peaches and melons into pieces of the same size. Place all the fruit in a bowl with the Grand Marnier and sugar; macerate for 30 minutes. Drain and set aside. Reserve juices.

To make the sauce: place the egg yolks, water, cream and sugar in the top of a double boiler. Whisk briskly over gently simmering water until the consistency of thick cream. Add the reserved juice a little at a time, whisking constantly.

Just before serving, arrange the fruit in a buttered gratin dish and cover with the cream sauce. Sprinkle a little sugar on top and place under a preheated broiler, set at maximum heat, until the sugar caramelizes. Serve at once.

INDONESIAN LUNCH
FOR TWELVE

Fish with Piquant Sauce

Spicy Beef

Javanese Chicken

Yellow Rice

Hard-boiled Eggs with Spicy Coconut Sauce

Chinese Cabbage with Garlic and Ginger

Beans Flavored with Cinnamon and Soy Sauce

Platter of Tropical Fruits

Spice Islands Coffee

I ndonesian food is ideal for serving at large gatherings because, traditionally, all the dishes are presented at one time, rather than in separate courses. Different combinations of spicy flavors contrast with each other and are balanced with rice.

The beef dish, a version of traditional lapis palaro, an Amboinese or Moluccan dish, is particularly hot – but the chilies can be reduced for timid taste buds. Cloves, nutmeg, coriander, cumin and ginger are also included. The chicken dish comes from Java, its flavor again being based on a heady combination of spices.

As Indonesia is comprised of about three thousand islands, there is fish in abundance. A dish easily adapted for occidental kitchens is lightly broiled fish, served with a piquant sauce of lime juice, chilies, ground ginger and lemon grass.

Chinese cabbage lightly fried with garlic and ginger; beans in a sweet-and-sour-style sauce flavored with cinnamon, soy sauce and coconut and hard-boiled eggs rolled in a spicy sauce are tasty accompaniments; the effect required is a melange of flavors. The perfect dessert, fresh tropical fruit.

Wine is not an every-day feature of Indonesian meals, being served only occasionally in the houses of the rich. Rather, a glass of water is consumed at the end of the meal, followed by tea. No liquid is ever consumed during the meal. Coffee can be enlivened with crushed cardamom seeds or a mixture of fresh nutmeg and black pepper.

Left: Spices from the East

FISH WITH PIQUANT SAUCE

Whole fish is quite delicious when broiled and served with this very special sauce. Choose from striped bass, sea bass or red snapper.

2 fish suitable for broiling (about 4 lb each),
  cleaned but with heads and tails left on
oil for broiling
1 shredded stalk of lemon grass or 3-inch
  piece of lemon rind, to garnish
sauce:
1 or 2 hot chilies, seeds removed
1 teaspoon crushed gingerroot

1 cup freshly squeezed lemon juice

To make the sauce: mix the chilies and the ginger with the lemon juice in a non-metallic bowl and allow to marinate overnight. Transfer to an airtight container and refrigerate.

To prepare the fish: slash each of them lightly at intervals on either side of the backbone and arrange them on a greased broiler rack. Make sure that they do not touch. Wrap fins and tails in foil. Brush lightly with oil and sprinkle with a little of the piquant sauce.

Place under a preheated broil and cook for about 15 minutes, turning carefully after 7 minutes and adding a little more piquant sauce from time to time. If any section of the fish becomes brown before the rest is cooked, cover it with foil. Test by probing with a fork – if the skin comes away from the flesh, the fish is cooked.

To serve: Transfer the cooked fish to a heated platter, garnish with lemon grass or lemon rind and serve with the remaining piquant sauce, strained into a sauce boat, in place of the more conventional lemon juice.

SPICY BEEF

This is a particularly hot dish, so the chilies may be reduced or even omitted to suit your taste.

¼ cup vegetable oil
3 lb chuck steak, cut into 2 × 1 × 1 inch
    chunks
1 cup canned coconut milk
1 tablespoon brown sugar
½ teaspoon freshly grated nutmeg
1 teaspoon coriander
½ teaspoon cumin
2 teaspoons freshly grated gingerroot
5 teaspoons soy sauce
6 chilies or to taste (optional)
1 tablespoon lemon juice
4 cloves
1 stick of cinnamon
2 tablespoons unsweetened shredded coconut,
    lightly toasted

Heat 3 tablespoons of the oil in a large frying pan. Add the meat, a few pieces at a time, and fry over moderate heat until browned. Using a slotted spoon, remove the meat chunks as they brown, and keep warm.

Put the coconut milk, brown sugar, nutmeg, coriander, cumin, ginger, soy sauce, chilies, lemon juice and 1 tablespoon oil in the container of a blender or food processor and process until well combined.

Pour the mixture into a large heavy-bottomed pan, add the reserved meat chunks and stir in the cloves, cinnamon stick and toasted coconut.

Cover the pan and cook on low heat for about 1¼ hours or until the meat is tender. Remove the lid for the last half hour of cooking to allow most of the liquid to evaporate. This is a fairly dry beef dish. Serve hot.

Left: Fish with piquant sauce
Above: Javanese chicken
Below: Spicy beef

JAVANESE CHICKEN

This dish is traditionally seasoned with ground laos, also known as galanga root, and is used in many Indonesian recipes. It is a member of the ginger family. If you are able to obtain it, decrease the grated gingerroot by 1 teaspoon and add 1 teaspoon laos.

1 tablespoon oil
3 lb chicken parts
2 large onions, diced
¾ lb tomatoes, peeled
1 teaspoon salt
2 teaspoons turmeric
4 cloves garlic, peeled
3 teaspoons grated gingerroot
3 chilies, seeded (optional)
2 teaspoons coriander
1 teaspoon cumin
1 cup canned coconut milk
1 tablespoon lemon juice
1 stalk lemon grass or 3-inch piece of lemon
    rind
2 cinnamon sticks
1 tablespoon unsweetened shredded coconut,
    lightly toasted

Heat the oil in a large frying pan. Add the chicken parts and fry over moderate heat until brown all over. Remove the chicken parts and set aside on paper towels.

Add the onion to the oil remaining in the pan and fry until golden. Remove with a slotted spoon and set aside.

Place all the remaining ingredients except for the lemon grass or rind, cinnamon sticks and toasted coconut in the container of a blender or food processor and process until well combined.

Pour the mixture into a large heavy-bottomed pan. Stir in the reserved onion and toasted coconut. Add the chicken parts, lemon grass or rind and cinnamon and stir thoroughly.

Bring the mixture to the boil, then reduce the heat and simmer for about 45 minutes until the chicken is very tender. Transfer to a serving dish and serve.

CHINESE CABBAGE WITH GARLIC AND GINGER

1 tablespoon oil
3 cloves garlic, chopped finely
1 tablespoon freshly grated gingerroot
1 Chinese cabbage, shredded
salt
freshly ground pepper
garnish:
fresh white bread crumbs
grated lemon rind

Heat the oil in a saucepan with the garlic and ginger. When the garlic has browned slightly, add the cabbage and salt and pepper. Toss and stir for about 3–5 minutes, until the cabbage is cooked but still crisp. Transfer to a serving dish and garnish with bread crumbs and lemon rind.

HARD-BOILED EGGS WITH SPICY COCONUT SAUCE

6 hard-boiled eggs
sauce:
2 large onions, chopped and fried
2 tablespoons unsweetened shredded coconut, toasted lightly
2 teaspoons turmeric
4 cloves garlic, crushed
¾ lb tomatoes, peeled
2 teaspoons coriander
1 teaspoon ground ginger
1 teaspoon cumin
1 teaspoon ground laos (see page 69)
1 cup canned coconut milk
1 stalk lemon grass or 1 tablespoon grated lemon rind

To make the sauce: place the onion and coconut in a heavy-bottomed pan, add all the remaining ingredients, except the eggs. Cook over moderate heat for 20 minutes, stirring occasionally.

Add the hard-boiled eggs and cook for 10 minutes more. The eggs taste better the longer they are left in the sauce, so if you have time, remove the pan from the heat and let it stand for a couple of hours before serving. Serve the eggs cold or reheat them gently.

YELLOW RICE

2 cups long-grain rice
4 cups canned coconut milk
2 teaspoons turmeric
24 black peppercorns
6 crushed cardamom pods
2 tablespoons oil
1 tablespoon butter
1 tablespoon chopped chives to garnish

Wash the rice in cold water. Drain, then place in a large heavy-bottomed saucepan with all the remaining ingredients (except the chives). Bring to the simmering point and cook for about 15 to 20 minutes over moderate heat until the rice is cooked. Spoon into a heated dish, top with chives and serve.

BEANS FLAVORED WITH CINNAMON AND SOY SAUCE

1 lb dried red kidney beans
¾ cup packed brown sugar
1 cinnamon stick
2 tablespoons soy sauce
1 tablespoon lemon juice
grated rind of ½ lemon
2 teaspoons unsweetened shredded coconut

Place the beans in a large earthenware bowl. Add all the remaining ingredients, except the coconut, and stir in 6 cups water. Allow the beans to soak overnight.

Next day, transfer the beans with the soaking liquid to a large saucepan and bring to the boil. Boil vigorously for 10 minutes to kill any toxins.

Add the coconut, reduce the heat and simmer the beans for about 1 hour or until tender. Serve hot.

Left: Hard-boiled eggs with spicy coconut sauce
Right: Chinese cabbage with garlic and ginger; Beans flavoured with cinnamon and soy sauce

SPICE ISLANDS COFFEE

Here are two quick ways to add flavor to your coffee.

Serve ordinary ground coffee with sugar to taste and float 10 crushed cardamom seeds on top before serving. Alternatively, sprinkle a mixture of grated fresh nutmeg and fresh ground black pepper over the coffee.

71

ITALIAN MEDLEY

FOR SIX

Iced Campari and Soda Served with Schiacciata con Ramerino

Risotto Tricolore

Pollastrino alla Diavola

Insalata Mista

Sfrappole

Italian Cheeses and Summer Fruits
Coffee

Try presenting very familiar ingredients in unfamiliar guises; it is all a question of appearances. An Italian theme ties a meal together. Italian food is essentially very simple, but it makes the most of fresh, beautiful ingredients.

This medley of recipes, particularly suitable for an outdoor summer lunch, should be preceded by icy Campari and soda, served with diamonds of schiacciata con ramerino, a delectable Italian bread sprinkled with fresh rosemary.

Risotto tricolore, colored in honor of the Italian flag, is an economical entrée that is visually stunning and highly appetizing; rice should never be written off as just an accompaniment. Grilled or broiled chicken is always popular particularly if it is cooked outdoors as guests can watch.

Sfrappole are deep-fried cookies made in bow shapes and presented dusted with sugar or drizzled with honey. Serve them with freshly made coffee.

Italian cheeses and fresh fruits complete the meal and enhance the atmosphere.

Left: A selection of Italian cheeses and summer fruits

SCHIACCIATA CON RAMERINO
(Italian Bread)

1 package active dry yeast
1 cup lukewarm water
2 cups all-purpose flour
salt
3 tablespoons olive oil
2 heaping tablespoons fresh rosemary leaves
freshly ground pepper

In a bowl, dissolve the yeast in the lukewarm water. Place all but 3 or 4 tablespoons of the flour in a mound on a pasta board. Make a well in the center and pour in the dissolved yeast and a pinch of salt. Using a fork, slowly incorporate the flour. Knead the dough for 15 minutes.

Sprinkle the dough with the remaining flour and cover with a cloth. Leave to stand in a warm place until doubled in size (about 1½ to 2 hours). When the dough has risen, oil a 15½ × 10½ × 1 inch jelly-roll pan with a tablespoon of the oil. Knock down the dough then place it in the pan and press it out until it covers the bottom.

Sprinkle on the rosemary, salt, lots of freshly ground pepper and the remaining oil. Cover and leave to stand until the dough has risen again to almost double size (about 1 hour).

Bake the schiacciata in a preheated 400° oven for about 30 to 40 minutes or until crisp. Remove from the pan, cut into diamonds and serve.

RISOTTO TRICOLORE

6 tablespoons butter
1 large onion, chopped finely
2 cups Arborio rice
1 cup dry white wine
8 cups chicken stock
3 tablespoons chopped Italian parsley
1 tablespoon chopped fresh basil
1 tablespoon tomato paste
1 cup freshly grated Parmesan cheese
salt
additional grated Parmesan cheese

Melt 3 tablespoons of the butter in a large saucepan and when the butter foams, add the onion. Sauté over medium heat until pale yellow. Add the rice and mix well. When the rice is coated with butter, add the wine. Cook, stirring constantly, until the wine has evaporated.

Stir in 1 or 2 cups of the stock and keep stirring until absorbed. Continue cooking and stirring the rice, adding stock a little at a time.

Divide the rice into 3 equal portions. Put 1 portion of rice into each of 2 small saucepans, leaving the third portion in the original one. Add the parsley and basil to 1 pan, the tomato paste to another and nothing to the third.

Continue cooking and stirring until the rice is tender but firm to the bite, add 1 tablespoon butter and a third of the Parmesan to each pan. Mix to blend and add salt to taste.

Arrange the rice in a large, warm serving dish with white rice in the middle and red and green on each side. Serve immediately with the additional grated Parmesan cheese.

Above left: Schiacciata con ramerino
Left: Risotto tricolore
Opposite right: Pollastrino alla diavola
Opposite far right: Insalata mista
Right: Sfrappole

74

POLLASTRINO ALLA DIAVOLA
(Broiled Cornish Hens)

6 Rock Cornish Hens
½ cup olive oil
salt
freshly ground pepper
2 cups Italian white wine
2 tablespoons lemon juice
garnish:
lemon slices
Italian parsley

Cut the Cornish Hens lengthwise along the backbone. Open out the Cornish hens until flat (or ask your butcher to do this for you). With a large cleaver or meat pounder, flatten without breaking the bones. Wash and dry thoroughly.

Combine the oil, salt, wine, lemon juice and plenty of pepper in a small bowl. Brush the Cornish hens on both sides with the oil mixture.

Place the birds in a large shallow dish, and pour the remaining oil mixture over. Leave to stand for 2 to 3 hours, basting several times.

Preheat the broiler or prepare the grill. Arrange the Cornish hens, skin side facing the heat. Cook for 10 to 15 minutes. Turn and baste with the marinade. Cook 10 to 15 minutes longer or until tender. Season with additional pepper. Place on a warm platter, garnish with lemon slices and parsley and serve.

INSALATA MISTA
(Mixed Salad)

Use the very best, fresh Italian vegetables such as baby radicchio, arugula, radishes and herbs to create a mixed salad.

SFRAPPOLE
(Italian Biscuits)

2 cups all-purpose flour
2 eggs
¼ cup butter
½ cup sugar
2 tablespoons rum
2 tablespoons chilled sweet white wine
oil for frying
powdered sugar or honey, to finish

Place the flour on a wooden board and make a well in the center. Break the eggs into the well and beat lightly with a fork. Add the butter, sugar, rum and wine and mix thoroughly with the eggs. Using your hands, gradually incorporate the flour, starting from the inside of the well. Work the dough into a ball. Cover and refrigerate for 20 to 25 minutes.

Roll out the dough on a lightly floured surface until ¼ inch thick. Using a pastry wheel or sharp knife, cut the dough into strips ¾ inch wide and 6 or 7 inches long. Tie the strips in knots or pin in bows.

Pour oil into a large saucepan or deep fryer until 2 inches deep. Heat the oil to 375°. Using a slotted spoon, lower the bows a few at a time into the hot oil. Turn the bows while cooking. When golden brown on both sides, remove and drain on paper towels. Arrange the bows on a platter and dust with powdered sugar, or drizzle with some honey.

WARMING LUNCH
──────────FOR SIX──────────

Parsnip Soup with Cheese Croutons

Glazed Ham

or

Veal Piedmontaise
Tagliatelle with Poppy Seeds
Tossed Green Salad with Hazelnut Vinaigrette

Pears in Coffee Syrup

Lunchtimes, particularly in the cooler months, are ideal for casual reunions with family and friends. Dishes that can be prepared ahead, reheated and then served with the minimum of fuss are a boon. The food itself can be a talking point, especially if it is innovative.

Take parsnips, for example, a much maligned vegetable. Few who have shivered in from the outdoors would not warm to a soup of parsnip, enlivened with a dash of curry and a toasted crouton of French bread topped with Gruyère cheese.

Baked ham, a long-time favorite at festive gatherings, is perfect for this sort of occasion as guests can help themselves, if necessary. A green salad tossed in hazelnut vinaigrette adds a crisp note of contrast.

The veal casserole is a step above the norm, too, as it incorporates Marsala, dried apricots and rosemary. Tagliatelle, which is fairly bland but has an interesting texture, always goes well with flavorsome thick cream sauces. This version shines because of the addition of toasted poppy seeds.

Pears in coffee sauce are a useful dessert because they need little last-minute garnishing, just a dash of whipped cream and grated chocolate. A fruit dessert is welcome after a bulky meal because it cleanses the palate, while still adding a sweet note.

Left: Tagliatelle with poppy seeds (page 79)

PARSNIP SOUP

½ cup butter
2 lb parsnips, peeled and cut in chunks
2 onions, chopped
1 teaspoon curry powder
10½-oz can beef consommé
water (see instructions)
1¼ cups cream
milk (see instructions)
salt
freshly ground pepper
garnish:
chopped chives
cheese croutons (recipe follows)

Melt the butter in a large heavy-bottomed saucepan. Add the parsnips and onions, cover and cook gently. Do not brown the vegetables but just let them absorb the butter. Add the curry powder, consommé and a consommé can full of water. Simmer gently until the vegetables are soft, about 20 minutes.

Purée in a blender or food processor. Return the mixture to the saucepan. Add the cream and as much milk as is necessary to achieve the desired consistency. Add salt and pepper to taste. Heat through and serve sprinkled with plenty of chopped chives. Pass the cheese croutons separately.

CHEESE CROUTONS

Spread slices of French bread liberally with slices of Gruyère cheese and place them on a baking sheet. Cook them in the center of a preheated 400° oven for about 10 minutes until the cheese has melted and the bread is crisp.

TOSSED GREEN SALAD

Simply create a mixed green salad using a variety of vegetables and toss in a well-seasoned vinaigrette made with hazelnut oil.

78

GLAZED HAM

1 cooked ham
prepared mustard
ground cloves
1 cup pineapple juice
$\frac{1}{4}$ cup sherry
1-lb package brown sugar

Strip the rind from the ham, rub the fat well with mustard and sprinkle with ground cloves. Stand the ham in a large baking dish and prop up each side with skewers, making the ham level so the top will not brown unevenly when you cook it.

Put the pineapple juice, sherry and brown sugar in a saucepan and bring it to the boil. Pour around, not over, the ham. Bake near the bottom of a preheated 300° oven for 30 minutes, then start basting and cook the ham for 1 more hour, turning the dish frequently to brown the ham evenly. Serve hot or cold.

Left: Parsnip soup with cheese croutons
Above: Pears in coffee syrup

VEAL PIEDMONTAISE

$\frac{1}{4}$ lb smoked ham, diced
3 tablespoons olive oil
1 onion, sliced
2 cloves garlic, crushed
3 lb trimmed neck or shoulder of veal, cut in
  2-inch cubes
2 teaspoons fresh rosemary leaves
3 tomatoes, peeled and sliced
$\frac{1}{2}$ lb mushrooms, sliced
$\frac{1}{2}$ cup dried apricots, cut in pieces
1$\frac{1}{2}$ cups consommé
3 tablespoons lemon juice
$\frac{1}{4}$ cup dry Marsala
2 egg yolks
$\frac{1}{4}$ cup cream
chopped parsley to garnish

Place the ham in a small pan, add water to cover and parboil for a few seconds. Drain and transfer to a deep, heavy flameproof casserole together with the olive oil, onion and garlic. Fry until brown. Add the veal and cook until seared or browned on all sides.

Sprinkle generously with rosemary, add tomatoes, mushrooms, apricots, consommé, lemon juice and Marsala. Simmer covered, over low heat, until the meat is tender, about 1 hour.

Just before serving, beat the egg yolks with the cream in a small bowl. Stir in 2 tablespoons of the veal stock, then add the yolk mixture to the casserole and stir for 2 to 3 minutes over low heat to thicken the sauce slightly. Do not allow the sauce to boil. Sprinkle with parsley and serve at once, with tagliatelle.

TAGLIATELLE WITH POPPY SEEDS

1 lb tagliatelle
$\frac{1}{2}$ cup butter, melted
seasoning salt
freshly ground pepper
1 tablespoon toasted poppy seeds

Cook the tagliatelle in a large pan of rapidly boiling water for about 10 to 12 minutes or until tender but still firm to the bite.

Drain and place the tagliatelle in a large warmed serving bowl. Add the remaining ingredients and toss well. Serve immediately.

PEARS IN COFFEE SYRUP

1 cup strong black coffee
$\frac{1}{2}$ cup sugar
6 pears
to decorate:
1$\frac{1}{4}$ cups heavy cream, whipped
grated chocolate

Make a syrup with the coffee and sugar: place them in a very large pan and heat gently, stirring, until the sugar has dissolved. Bring to the boil and boil for 5 minutes without stirring.

Peel the pears, leaving the stems on, and stand them in the syrup. Cover and simmer gently for 15 to 20 minutes or until they are cooked. Lift out the pears and arrange them in a large shallow serving dish.

Boil the coffee syrup and reduce until it thickens. Then remove it from the heat and set it aside to cool. When quite cool, pour it over the pears, cover and chill.
To serve: cover the pears with whipped cream and sprinkle with plenty of grated chocolate.

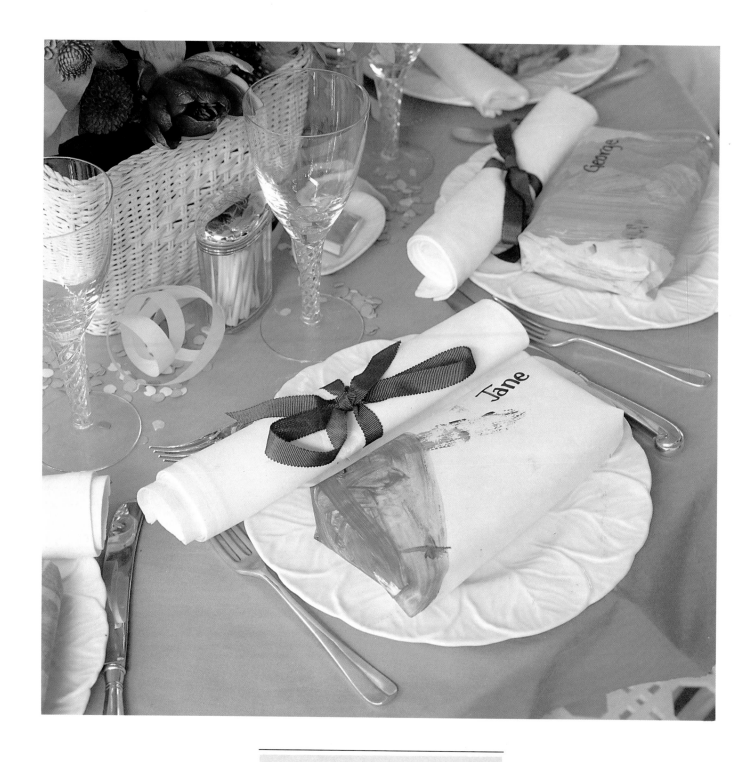

Veal with Tuna Mayonnaise
or
Gingered Beef Tongue
Jambon Persillé
Pasta Salad with Eggplant and Basil
Crisp Green Salad
French Bread

Chocolate Cake

BIRTHDAY BUFFET
————FOR TEN OR TWELVE————

I n summer, an informal celebration served outdoors – in the garden, on the terrace or by the pool – can have a picnic air. Light food is the order of the day as are dishes that can be shared buffet-style and adapt well to any number of guests. Crisp green salads can be served with a medley of meat dishes.

Veal with tuna mayonnaise has been adapted from the well-known Italian dish, vitello tonnato, in which veal fillets have been used instead of a whole piece of rolled veal. The contrasting flavors of veal and tuna-laced mayonnaise make this a tangy dish.

Jambon Persillé, another classic, is a jellied concoction of ham in a well-flavored sauce. Because this has to set, it must be made the day before so it can be sliced easily when serving. Gingered beef tongue, a variation of an old favorite, is an alternative dish that goes well with this line-up.

Pasta salad is a useful addition to the buffet spread because its texture contrasts with the meat dishes and standard green salad. Artichoke hearts, dried tomatoes, eggplants and basil conspire to give the dish a Mediterranean feel and it is perfectly complemented by the two European meat dishes.

Rich moist chocolate cake is universally popular. At a large informal gathering it comes into its own because, like the rest of this menu, it can be made ahead and served very easily.

Left: Setting the scene for a birthday buffet

VEAL WITH TUNA MAYONNAISE

2 veal fillets weighing about 1½ lb each
butter
tuna mayonnaise:
1 tablespoon Dijon mustard
2 or 3 tablespoons lemon juice
4 egg yolks
freshly ground pepper
1½ cups olive oil
2-oz can anchovy fillets
6½-oz can tuna
capers to garnish

Trim the veal fillets. Heat the butter in a frying pan and lightly brown the fillets. Transfer to a roasting pan and roast in a preheated 375° oven for 20–25 minutes. Cool completely.

To make the mayonnaise: place the mustard, lemon juice, egg yolks and pepper in a blender or food processor and process well. With the motor still running, gradually add the olive oil. Process the anchovy and tuna and add to the mixture. Cover the veal with a quarter of the mayonnaise. Place in a china dish and cover with plastic wrap. Leave overnight in the refrigerator.

Next day, scrape off the sauce and thinly slice the veal. Arrange slices of the veal on a serving dish, pour the remaining sauce over the slices and garnish with capers.

Left: Veal with tuna mayonnaise

GINGERED BEEF TONGUE

2 smoked beef tongues
6 garlic cloves
8 slices peeled fresh ginger
2 tablespoons brown sugar
2 tablespoons vinegar
water

Wash the tongues well under cold water. Place in a very large casserole with the garlic, ginger, brown sugar and vinegar. Pour in enough water to fill the pan. Bring to the boil, cover and simmer for $3\frac{1}{2}$ hours. Taste the water after 1 hour and, if very salty, drain it off and replace with fresh water.

When the tongues are cooked, remove from the water, peel off the skin and cut away any coarse meat. Remove the ginger from the cooking water and cut in fine slivers.

Arrange the tongues in a bowl or oblong pan, sprinkling with the slivered ginger as you do so. Weight firmly with a board and heavy weights (such as cans of food lying sideways), as if pressing a terrine. Cover and refrigerate for 24 hours. Serve sliced thinly with a good fruit chutney.

JAMBON PERSILLÉ

$\frac{1}{2}$ a cooked ham, about 10 lb
stock:
4 lb veal neck and breast bones
2 pig's feet
handful of parsley stems
1 lemon, cut into quarters
2 carrots, peeled and chopped
2 celery stalks, chopped
2 onions, peeled and chopped
3 garlic cloves
sprig of thyme
freshly ground pepper
1 × 750 ml bottle dry white wine
1 quart water
to assemble:
jellied stock (see instructions)
1 envelope gelatin, softened
$1\frac{1}{2}$ cups chopped parsley
freshly ground pepper
$\frac{1}{2}$ cup chopped parsley to garnish

Remove the rind from the ham. Cut the meat from the bone in large pieces. Trim off any dried smoked ham and most of the thick fat and discard. Cut the ham into $1\frac{1}{2}$–2-inch dice. Cover and refrigerate.

To make the stock: place all the ingredients in a large pan, cover, bring to the boil and simmer until the meat falls off the bones.

Strain the stock. Pick the meat from the pig's feet and reserve. Discard the bones and vegetables. Stand the stock in the refrigerator overnight to set the fat.

To assemble: remove the fat from the stock, then place the stock in a large pan and bring to a simmer. Add the meat from the pig's feet and the diced ham. Simmer gently, covered, for 30 minutes. Remove from the heat, add the gelatin and stir until dissolved. Add the parsley and pepper to taste (there will be enough salt in the ham).

Pour the mixture into one or two large loaf pans or a large white bowl. Allow to cool then cover and refrigerate overnight.

To serve: if using loaf pans, turn the jambon persillé out on to one or two serving platters and garnish with a row of parsley. If using a large white bowl, simply sprinkle the parsley over the top and allow your guests to cut slices straight from the bowl.

CHOCOLATE CAKE

6 eggs
1 cup caster sugar
7 tablespoons all-purpose flour
7 tablespoons cocoa
½ cup melted, clarified butter, cooled
butter cream:
4 egg yolks
½ cup sugar
scant ½ cup water
1 cup unsalted butter, softened
chocolate glaze:
4 oz semisweet chocolate
3 tablespoons unsalted butter

To make the cake: butter and line a 9-inch square cake pan. Place the eggs and sugar in a bowl and using an electric mixer beat until the mixture holds stiff peaks. Sift together the flour and cocoa. Fold into the mixture with a metal spoon and when almost incorporated, add the clarified butter and gently mix.

Spoon the mixture into the prepared pan and bake in a preheated 350° oven until firm to touch, or when tested with a skewer it comes away clean. Turn out on to a wire rack and leave to cool.

To make the butter cream: using an electric mixer, beat the egg yolks until pale and thick. Place the sugar and water in a saucepan and heat gently, stirring frequently until the sugar dissolves. Bring to the boil and boil the syrup until it reads 240° on a candy thermometer or until it reaches soft ball stage (when a little syrup is dropped into cold water it will form a soft ball between your fingers). Gradually pour the hot syrup into the yolks, beating constantly, and continue beating until the mixture cools. Beat the softened butter into the mixture a little at a time.

To make the chocolate glaze: melt the chocolate in a double boiler, add the butter and beat well. Cool until the mixture is a spreadable consistency.

To assemble: slice the cake to give two layers and spread the butter cream thickly between the layers. Cover the cake with the chocolate glaze, smoothing the surface with a knife.

Note: A little liqueur or chopped nuts can be added to the butter cream.

PASTA SALAD WITH EGGPLANT AND BASIL

2 medium eggplants
salt
8 tablespoons olive oil
2 large onions, sliced
4 ripe tomatoes, peeled, seeded and chopped
2 sweet red peppers, sliced
½ lb button mushrooms
basil leaves to taste
¾ lb mixed white and green fettuccine
1 14-oz can artichoke hearts, drained and halved
½ lb jar pomodori secchi (Italian dried tomatoes in oil)
additional shredded basil leaves to taste
freshly ground pepper

Cut the eggplants into 1-inch cubes. Salt and allow to stand for 2 hours to sweat. Pat dry with a paper towel.

Heat the oil in a pan and gently fry the onions until soft. Add the chopped tomatoes and cook until the mixture thickens. Add the cubed eggplant and cook until soft. Add the red peppers, mushrooms and basil. Cook for a further 5 minutes.

Cook the pasta in a large saucepan of boiling salted water. Drain and refresh under cold running water. Drain well, shaking the colander to remove as much excess water as possible.

Toss the pasta with the eggplant mixture. Add the artichokes, sliced dried tomatoes, oil from the jar and shredded basil leaves. Taste for salt and pepper and turn into a serving bowl. Serve the salad at room temperature.

Far left: Jambon persillé
Above: Pasta salad with eggplant and basil

83

COME TO DINNER

If you ask the worldly-wise among your friends what kind of gathering they most enjoy, nine times out of ten the answer will be a little dinner for six or eight people.

Chosen carefully and encouraged by good food and wine, a group of that size will produce conviviality and conversation that goes beyond the superficial chitchat of the cocktail party.

Now is the time to bring on your best in culinary accomplishments and artful settings. Light the candles, play the music, set the table with imagination, dress in something special, but save your greatest skills for the kitchen. Finesse and freshness should be of paramount importance.

The other essential is your presence with your guests and if that means enlisting hired help in the kitchen and at the table, go ahead. Your absence will not make your guests grow fonder; on the contrary, it will make them ill at ease.

To bring off this kind of occasion with full success you need to pre-plan. It's not the kind of thing to be sandwiched into a full working day. Save it for those times when you're free to enjoy the anticipation, preparation and culmination of your own exquisite little dinner party.

Mussel and Leek Tarts with Saffron Sauce

Fish Braids with Tomato Basil Sauce

Fillets of Lamb with Beet Confits
Vegetable Timbales

Kumquat Bavarois
Brandy Snap Horns

ELEGANT DINNER
FOR TWELVE

T his is an original dinner menu, using methods evolved from classical culinary techniques. The emphasis is on unusual combinations of flavors and fresh seasonal ingredients. As is generally necessary with formal dinners, much of the preparation can be done the day beforehand.

Brandied kumquats, which are used as a garnish for the dessert, can be made by the organized cook when the fruit is in season. They must be stored for six months before use. However, the crunchy brandy snap horns should be made the day they are served.

At a formal dinner, opt to serve two contrasting courses before the main – in this case a mussel and leek tart served in a saffron and champagne sauce and a graphic braid of pink and white fish.

Lamb and beets are not usually thought of as a duo, but the main course proves that they can work well together. In this case, boned lamb loins are briefly cooked in a hearty stock and then served with a rich jamlike beet mass.

A light dessert, such as a bavarois, should be served to refresh the palate after a heavy meat course.

Left: Fish braids with tomato basil sauce (page 88)
Above: Mussel and leek tart with saffron sauce

MUSSEL AND LEEK TARTS WITH CHAMPAGNE SAUCE

½ lb package frozen puff pastry
3 lb mussels
sauce:
1 teaspoon saffron threads
1 cup mussel liquor (see instructions)
1½ cups good quality brut Champagne
2½ cups cream
leek filling:
7 tablespoons butter
3 leeks, white part only, sliced finely
1 cup mussel liquor (see instructions)

To make the tart shells: thaw 1 sheet of pastry and roll out thin enough to line the tart pans. Cut out 6 to 8 circles and line lightly oiled 3-inch tart pans with pastry, making sure pastry extends over tops to allow for shrinkage. Line tart shells with circles of waxed paper and fill with dried beans. Place the tart shells in a preheated 425° oven and bake for 20 minutes. Remove beans and paper and carefully lift out tart shells. Return shells to a turned-off or very low oven to dry and crisp.

To cook the mussels: scrub and de-beard mussels and soak them in several changes of cold water for 2 hours. Place the drained mussels in a large frying pan with a tight-fitting lid and set over a high heat. Give the pan a vigorous shake after 2 to 3 minutes. The mussels should have opened after 5 minutes. Discard any unopened mussels. Remove the mussels from their shells and set them aside. Strain the mussel liquor through a tamis or cheesecloth and reserve. Taste the liquor; if it is excessively salty do not add a full cup to the sauce or the leeks.

To make the sauce: start making the sauce about 30 minutes before serving. Combine the saffron, up to 1 cup mussel liquor, the Champagne and the cream in a heavy-bottomed saucepan and boil gently until reduced by half.

To cook the leeks: melt the butter in a small saucepan and sauté the leeks for a few minutes. Add up to 1 cup mussel liquor and boil rapidly for 5 minutes. Drain and keep warm.

To assemble: fill each tart shell with mussels. Reheat in a preheated 350° oven for 5 minutes. Remove the tarts from the oven and spoon about 1 heaping tablespoon of leeks into each one. Place the tarts on heated individual serving plates, surround with the hot Champagne sauce and serve immediately.

FISH BRAIDS WITH TOMATO BASIL SAUCE

These fish braids look extremely attractive. To make them, you will require 6 sheets of firm cardboard, each measuring 8 × 4 inches, covered with foil.

tomato basil sauce:
4 large ripe tomatoes
3 cups concentrated fish stock
1 cup dry white wine
1¼ cups cream whisked with 2 egg yolks (optional)
1 cup finely shredded fresh basil

fish plaits:
3 fillets sole, skinned, the same length as the trout fillets
6 fillets pink rainbow trout, skinned
2 tablespoons softened butter
freshly ground pepper
2 cups white wine or good fish stock

To make the sauce: peel, seed and core the tomatoes. Do not discard the peelings. Cut the tomato flesh into fine dice and reserve. Place the skins, seeds and cores in a saucepan with the fish stock and wine and boil until the liquid is reduced by half. Strain the sauce into a clean pan, discarding the solids that remain in the strainer. Cool slightly. For a thicker sauce, stir the cream and egg yolks into the reduced stock. Add the chopped tomatoes and basil. The tomato should be heated through gently so that it still retains its fresh raw taste.

To cook the fish: cut the fillets in half lengthwise to make 18 strips. Butter the prepared foil-covered cardboard sheets well, then, using 1 white and 2 pink strips of fish, make a braid directly on each sheet.

Lay the sheets in a single layer in a large baking dish, pepper lightly and pour in the white wine or fish stock. Cover the dish tightly with foil and bake in a preheated 400° to 425° oven for 8 to 10 minutes, until the fish is just cooked.

To serve: reheat the sauce if necessary (do not allow it to boil). Pour a little of the hot sauce on to each plate and slide a fish braid carefully on to the sauce. Serve immediately.

Above: Fillets of lamb with beet confits

FILLETS OF LAMB WITH BEET CONFITS

Ask your butcher to bone 3 lamb loins containing 6 chops each. Reserve bones for stock and the small fillets for another dish. (If you save bones in your freezer for making soup, you will need about 2 lb to make this stock.)

3 boned lamb loins, as above
stock:
1 veal knuckle, sawed in pieces
reserved lamb bones and meat scraps
1 beet, chopped
3 onions, peeled and chopped
2 carrots, chopped
2 tomatoes, chopped
8 cloves garlic, halved
red wine (see instructions)
water (see instructions)
several sprigs of fresh thyme
sprig of fresh rosemary
bouquet garni
1 tablespoon white peppercorns
beet confits:
¼ cup butter
3 beets, peeled and cut in julienne (matchstick) strips
1 cup lamb stock, as above
juice of 1 orange
1 teaspoon fresh thyme

freshly ground pepper
sauce:
2 cups lamb stock, as above
1 cup red wine
¾ cup plus 2 tablespoons butter
garnish:
boiled baby beets

To make the stock: place the veal pieces, lamb bones and meat scraps, beets, onions, carrots, tomatoes and garlic in a large baking pan and roast in a 400° oven until well browned.

Transfer to a large saucepan and cover with equal parts of red wine and water. Add the herbs and peppercorns. Bring slowly to the boil, reduce the heat and simmer gently. Skim frequently during the first 15 minutes and cook slowly until the meat is falling off the bones (about 5 to 6 hours).

You may have to add a little more wine and water while the stock is cooking. The stock should be very strong but you must have about 2 quarts of stock to cook the lamb, beets and sauce.

When the stock is cooked, strain, cool and refrigerate to set the fat. Remove the fat from the surface and discard.

To cook the beet confits: melt the butter in a saucepan. Add the beetroot strips, cover and sweat gently. Add the stock, orange juice, thyme, and pepper to taste. Simmer for 30 minutes until the beets are tender and the mixture resembles jam. Set aside in a warm place.

To make the sauce: put the lamb stock and red wine in a saucepan and boil until well reduced. Turn off the heat and reserve the butter to whisk into the sauce just before serving. (The sauce will not reheat after the butter has been added.)

To cook the lamb fillets: bring at least 1 quart of the stock to a full rolling boil in a large pot or fish poacher with a lid. Have the fillets at room temperature. Place in the boiling stock, cover and cook for 4 minutes if you want to serve rare or pink lamb and 5 minutes for medium-rare lamb. Remove the fillets to a board, cover with foil and allow to rest for a few minutes before serving.

To serve: reheat the sauce and beat in the butter a little at a time. Reheat the beets if necessary. Slice the fillets. Pour a little sauce on each plate and place slices of lamb on top. Serve a spoonful of beet confits on one side of the plate and garnish with 2 boiled and peeled baby beets.

VEGETABLE TIMBALES

Use two varieties of vegetable for the timbales – the choice is up to you. Some possible combinations include: sweet potato and carrots; parsnip and kohlrabi; Jerusalem artichokes and turnips; celeriac and potatoes.

2 cups vegetable purée (2 varieties – 1 cup of each)
4 eggs
2 scant cups cream
grated nutmeg
salt
freshly ground pepper

Place the vegetable purées in separate bowls. To each mix in 2 beaten eggs and 1 scant cup cream. Flavor with nutmeg, salt and pepper.

Butter 6 small china molds. Spoon the purées into the moulds in layers. Place the molds in a baking dish and pour in boiling water to come halfway up the sides of the molds. Cover with buttered waxed paper. Cook in a preheated 400° oven for 40 minutes. Remove the timbales from the water bath and rest for 5 minutes before unmolding.

KUMQUAT BAVAROIS
(Makes 12 small molds)

1⅔ cups milk
4 egg yolks
4 tablespoons sugar
1½ tablespoons gelatin, softened in 2 tablespoons water
¾ cup kumquat purée
1⅓ cups heavy cream
½ cup kumquat brandy (see brandied kumquats below)
to decorate:
1 cup heavy cream, whipped
sugar
brandy snap horns (recipe follows)
brandied kumquats (recipe follows)

Using a heavy-bottomed saucepan, bring the milk to the boil. Meanwhile, beat the yolks and sugar together until well mixed. Slowly add the hot milk, whisking constantly. Return the mixture to the pan and cook over low heat, whisking constantly, until the mixture coats the back of a spoon.

Add the gelatin to the hot custard and stir well until dissolved. Add the kumquat purée. Allow the mixture to cool, whisking from time to time.

Whip the cream with the kumquat brandy until stiff. As the custard cools it thickens; when it is as thick as the whipped cream, fold in the whipped cream. (The custard will thicken more quickly if you set it in a bowl of ice.) Pour the mixture into the molds and set in the refrigerator overnight.

To serve: sweeten the whipped cream with sugar to taste, cover and refrigerate until required. Pipe rosettes of cream into the brandy snap horns just before serving and decorate with brandied kumquats.

BRANDIED KUMQUATS

This is a technique which requires common sense rather than specific quantities.

Wash a large preserving jar and sterilize it by placing it in a 300° oven for 30 minutes. Wash the kumquats and prick them all over with a darning needle. Layer kumquats in the jar. To each layer of fruit add approximately ½ cup superfine sugar. Alternate layers of fruit with brandy. Seal and store for at least 6 months in a cool place before opening.

Use the preserved kumquats as decoration and use the drained brandy to flavor the kumquat bavarois.

BRANDY SNAP HORNS

The brandy snap mixture can be made up to 1 week before it is baked. Store it, well-covered, in the refrigerator.

¾ cup unsalted butter
¼ cup maple syrup
1 tablespoon brandy
1 cup all-purpose flour
¾ cup sugar
1 tablespoon ginger juice made by forcing small pieces of fresh ginger through a garlic press
⅓ cup pecans, crushed finely in a food processor

Melt the butter over low heat and add the maple syrup and brandy. Remove from the heat and add the flour, sugar, ginger juice and pecans. Stir thoroughly to combine.

Drop 1 tablespoon of mixture at a time on to a greased baking sheet at least 6 inches apart to allow for spreading.

Bake in a preheated 325–350° oven until golden, about 10 minutes. Remove from the oven and allow to rest a few seconds. Quickly lift with a spatula and roll into horn shapes around the handles of wooden spoons. Store in an airtight container.

Left: Kumquat bavarois with brandied kumquat and brandy snap horns

INDIAN FEAST
——— FOR TWELVE ———

Ginger Prawns

Chapati

Spiced Almond Chicken

Spinach Rice

Sambals

Mariel Samosas

Cinnamon Tea

L ike India itself, Indian cooking is a mix of wonderful colors and sensations. Particularly suitable for informal dinner parties, the food in this menu can be served either all at once, in the traditional manner or in courses. Either way, the sambals should remain on the table for the duration of the meal because they offer a balance of hot and cold flavors that can be blended with the main dishes as desired.

Some of the food can be cooked on a traditional Indian grill (if you are lucky enough to own one) and much of it can be prepared in advance. The chapati dough, for example, can be made ahead and then cooked at the last minute. Take care when preparing this puffy unleavened bread; if punctured, the pieces will not rise.

Garam masala, a mixture of several spices used in many recipes, is better if you grind it yourself. Whole spices are on sale in specialty stores. A small coffee grinder fulfils the purpose and should be kept specially for spice grinding.

The spiced almond chicken is a Kashmiri dish. Spicy rather than hot, it is marinated for 24 hours before cooking and is served with the rich pan juices and tasty spinach rice.

Wine is rarely served with Indian food as the tastes are not really complementary. However, cinnamon tea proves to be a refreshing drink if served after eating.

Left: A selection of sambals (pages 94/95)

GINGER PRAWNS

2 lb fresh green prawns
½ cup vegetable oil
3 tablespoons lemon juice
1 medium onion, chopped roughly
6 cloves garlic, chopped roughly
1½-inch piece fresh ginger
2 hot green chilies or 1 teaspoon chili powder
salt
freshly ground pepper

garnish:
lemon wedges
Vietnamese mint

Shell the prawns leaving the tail tips. Slit the backs of the prawns and remove the digestive tracts. Thread on 8 skewers.

Place 2 tablespoons of the oil in a blender or food processor, together with all the remaining ingredients except the garnish. Purée to a smooth paste. Spread the prawns with the paste and marinate in the refrigerator for at least 1 hour.

Cook over the hot grill or under a preheated broiler, turning once and brushing with the remaining oil until cooked. Serve with lemon and Vietnamese mint.

Below: Ginger prawns
Right: Spiced almond chicken

SPICED ALMOND CHICKEN

8 small chicken breasts on the bone
juice of 1½ lemons
2 teaspoons salt
1 teaspoon cayenne pepper
marinade:
½ cup raisins
⅔ cup flaked almonds
1 tablespoon clear honey
2 cloves garlic
2-inch piece of gingerroot, peeled and chopped
½ teaspoon cardamom pods
½ teaspoon cumin seeds
1 teaspoon turmeric
⅔ cup yogurt
½ cup cream
to cook chicken:
¼ teaspoon saffron threads, soaked in 2

tablespoons boiling water for 10 minutes
¼ cup butter, melted

Remove wings and skin from breasts, and make diagonal slits in each breast. In a small bowl, combine the lemon juice, salt and cayenne and rub this mixture all over chicken, especially into the slits. Put the chicken breasts side by side in a shallow dish. Set aside for 30 minutes.
To make the marinade: put the raisins, almonds, honey, garlic, ginger and spices into a blender with 4 tablespoons of the yogurt, and blend to a smooth purée. Transfer the purée to a bowl and beat in the remaining yogurt and the cream. Pour over the chicken, cover and chill in the refrigerator for 24 hours, turning the

chicken breasts occasionally.

Next day remove the chicken and marinade from the refrigerator and set it aside at room temperature for 1 hour.
To cook the chicken: drain the chicken, reserving the marinade, and arrange the breasts in a deep roasting pan. Combine the saffron mixture with the reserved marinade and pour it over the chicken. Spoon a little of the melted butter over the top.

Roast the chicken in a preheated 400° oven for 30 minutes or until tender, basting frequently with the remaining melted butter and the liquid in the pan. If the marinade starts to dry out, add a small quantity of water.

Transfer the chicken to a warmed serving dish. Spoon the pan juices over the chicken and serve with spinach rice and sambals.

SPINACH RICE

cooking liquid:
2 cups beef or veal stock
1 medium onion, quartered
4 cloves garlic
7 whole cloves
4 cardamom pods
2 teaspoons whole fennel seeds
1 teaspoon cumin seeds
1 teaspoon coriander seeds
1 stick of cinnamon
6 black peppercorns
1 bay leaf
spinach rice:
¾ cup Basmati rice
6 tablespoons vegetable oil
1 teaspoon garam masala (page 94)

2 onions, chopped finely
2 10-oz packages frozen spinach, thawed and
   squeezed dry
garnish:
16 onion rings deep fried in ghee (clarified
   butter) or oil

To prepare the cooking liquid: place the stock in a large heavy-bottomed saucepan. Wrap the remaining ingredients in a piece of cheesecloth, form it into a bag, tie the neck with string and lower it into the pan.

Bring the stock to the boil, cover, lower the heat, and simmer for 30 minutes. Remove the cheesecloth bag, squeezing the juices back into the pan. Pour the stock into a measuring cup and make up to 2 cups by adding water if necessary. Cool.

To cook the rice: wash the rice three times in cold water. Place in a heavy-bottomed pan with the cold stock. Bring to the boil, lower the heat, cover and simmer for 25 minutes. Turn off the heat but do not remove the pan from the stove.

To prepare the spinach rice: heat the oil in a heavy frying pan, add garam masala and sauté for 5 minutes. Add onions and cook until soft. Add the spinach and stir to heat through.

Fold the onion-spinach mixture into the drained hot rice, place it in a serving bowl and garnish with the crisply fried onion rings.

93

CHAPATI
(Makes 16)

You can buy chapati flour from most Asian food stores. If unavailable, substitute finely milled whole wheat flour or a mixture of half whole wheat and half all-purpose flour. The dough may be made up to 24 hours before it is baked provided it is kept wrapped in the refrigerator.

1⅔ cups chapati flour or whole wheat flour
about ¾ cup cold water
1 cup whole wheat flour for dusting the work surface
butter to cook chapati

Place the flour in a food processor and, with the machine in operation, gradually add the water until the mixture forms a ball. Alternatively, place the flour in a large bowl, and gradually add enough water until you can gather the mixture together into a ball. Knead the dough by hand for 7 minutes. Wrap in plastic wrap and refrigerate for at least 30 minutes.

Heat a heavy cast iron pan and the grill or broiler. Knead the dough again, divide into 16 balls and pat or roll into thin circles. Keep work surfaces well dusted with flour.

When the pan and grill or broiler are very hot, grease the pan lightly with butter and cook the chapati, a few at a time for 30 seconds, when they will start to bubble.

Turn the chapati carefully with flat-edged tongs or use your fingers. If chapati are punctured by heat or tongs, they will not puff. Cook for a further 30 seconds. The breads should have light brown spots on both sides.

Transfer the chapati to the grill or preheated broiler and they will puff immediately. Turn, cook for a few more seconds.

Butter the pan again and cook the remaining chapati in the same way. Serve hot.

GARAM MASALA

This is a mixture of several spices which is used in many Indian dishes. The combinations do vary, and prepared garam masala is available at Asian food stores and supermarkets, but this is the recipe used for the spinach rice in this menu.

3 tablespoons black peppercorns, ground
1 tablespoon ground cumin
1 teaspoon ground cinnamon
2 teaspoons ground cardamom
3 tablespoons ground coriander
1 teaspoon ground cloves
1½ teaspoons ground mace
¼ teaspoon grated nutmeg

Combine all the ingredients and store, tightly covered, in a cool dry place.

SAMBALS

Sambals (side dishes) are served at any Indian meal to offer a balance of hot and cold flavors. The guests help themselves according to individual taste. We suggest you serve cucumber raita, spicy shrimp sambal, mint raita and mango chutney (recipes follow).

Above: Chapati

94

CUCUMBER RAITA

2½ cups yogurt
½ cucumber, washed and diced
4 green onions, chopped finely
salt
freshly ground pepper
¼ teaspoon paprika

In a bowl, beat the yogurt until it is smooth, then fold in the cucumber, green onions, salt and pepper. Spoon into a serving bowl, cover and chill in the refrigerator for 1 hour. Sprinkle with paprika before serving.

MINT RAITA

1 bunch of mint
yogurt to bind
green food coloring

Chop the mint leaves, place in a bowl and add enough yogurt to bind. Stir and color as liked. Cover and chill until required. Sprinkle with a little extra chopped mint before serving.

SPICY SHRIMP SAMBAL

½ lb shrimps, cooked, shelled and chopped
2 hard-boiled eggs, sliced
1 medium onion, chopped finely
1 green chili, chopped and seeds removed
1-inch piece gingerroot, peeled and chopped
½ teaspoon hot chili powder
2 tablespoons thick coconut milk
¼ teaspoon cumin seeds, crushed coarsely

Combine all the ingredients except the cumin seeds and spoon into a shallow serving bowl. Sprinkle with cumin, cover and chill in refrigerator until required.

MANGO CHUTNEY
(Makes about two 1-quart jars)

3 lb green mangoes, peeled, halved and pitted
5 tablespoons salt
8¾ cups water
2½ cups (1 lb) sugar
2½ cups white wine vinegar
2-inch piece gingerroot, peeled and chopped
6 cloves garlic, crushed
2 teaspoons hot chili powder
1 cinnamon stick
1 cup pitted dates
1 cup raisins

Chop the mango flesh finely and put in a bowl. Add the salt and water. Cover and

set aside in a cool place for 24 hours.

Place sugar and vinegar in a large heavy-bottomed saucepan and bring to the boil, stirring until the sugar has dissolved. Strain the mangoes, discard the juice and add them to the sugar-vinegar syrup. Add the remaining ingredients and bring to the boil, stirring frequently.

Reduce the heat and simmer, stirring occasionally, for about 1½ hours or until the chutney is very thick. Remove the cinnamon stick and ladle the chutney into warmed, sterilized jars. Cover, label and store until required.

MARIEL SAMOSAS

The samosas can be prepared to the point of baking on the day before they are required. Store them, covered in plastic wrap, in the refrigerator.

12 oz frozen puff pastry, thawed
1 egg white, lightly beaten
filling:
¾ cup unsweetened grated coconut, soaked in
⅓ cup milk
½ teaspoon crushed cardamom seeds
⅓ cup sultanas

Above: Mariel samosas

¼ cup packed brown sugar
6 pieces crystallized ginger, chopped finely

To make the filling: combine the coconut, cardamom, sultanas, sugar and ginger.
To make the samosas: roll out the pastry on a floured board and cut into circles about 3 inches in diameter. Place a teaspoonful of the filling in the center of each circle and dampen the edges with water. Fold dough over and crimp with your fingers to seal. Place the pastries on lightly greased baking sheets, cover with plastic wrap and refrigerate for about 1 hour or overnight if preferred.
To cook: brush with egg white and bake in a preheated 425° oven for 20 minutes or until crisp and brown. Serve hot with cinnamon tea (recipe follows).

CINNAMON TEA

Simmer 2 cinnamon sticks in 9 cups of water for 20 minutes. Remove cinnamon and use the flavored water to make tea.

95

Beluga Caviar
East-West Hors d'Oeuvres

Cailles à la Normande sur Canapé
Jardinière de Petits Pois

Brie with Grapes and Walnuts

Tartelettes au Cointreau

BLACK TIE DINNER
——FOR SIX——

Influences from India and the Orient add subtlety to both the presentation and the dishes of this black tie dinner. Although the food is inspired by traditional French regional cooking, exotic spices are used as enlivening touches.

Truffles, arranged to resemble Chinese calligraphy, accent the cultural blend in East-West hors d'oeuvres. The truffles and lobster are surrounded by petal-like slices of mango and avocado and then highlighted with a curry mustard sauce.

Normandy-style quail are the feature of the main course. Stuffed with lumps of herb-and-garlic butter, the quail are broiled, flamed with Calvados and port, then just before serving they are brushed with honey for a sweet, crisp, golden-brown finish. Peas flavored with bacon, carrot and onion, and croûtons spread with thick dairy cream and roasted in the oven until crisp are served as accompaniments.

With the port, a wedge of Brie, fresh grapes and walnuts are served, followed by tartelettes au Cointreau, sweet pastry shells filled with orange-lemon cream and garnished with orange segments soaked in Cointreau. The perfect finale: rich chocolates, espresso coffee and a very old Cognac.

Left: Setting the scene for a black tie dinner

BELUGA CAVIAR

The evening begins with a touch of luxury: champagne and Beluga caviar served on sliced white bread that has been cut into rounds with a small cutter or brandy glass.

EAST-WEST HORS D'OEUVRES

2 or 3 cooked, cleaned lobster tails (according to size)
3 mangoes
3 avocados
curry mustard sauce:
3 teaspoons Dijon mustard
2 teaspoons Indian curry powder
2 teaspoons red wine vinegar
6 tablespoons peanut oil
garnish:
1-oz can truffles, drained

Slice the lobster tails in medallions – you will need 2 medallions per person. Peel and slice the mangoes and avocados in thin slices.
To make the mustard sauce: place the mustard, curry powder and vinegar in a small bowl and beat with a whisk. Gradually whisk in the oil, a few drops at a time, until the sauce is thick.
To serve: arrange hors d'oeuvres on black or blue-colored plates. Place 2 medallions of lobster in center of each plate and arrange alternating slices of mango and avocado as flower petals around medallions. Place a spoonful of mustard sauce on the lobster and garnish with a few julienne (matchstick) strips of truffle.

Left: Beluga caviar and Champagne

CAILLES À LA NORMANDE SUR CANAPÉ
(Normandy-style Quail)

JARDINIÈRE DE PETITS POIS

12 quail
½ cup butter
2 teaspoons chopped fresh thyme
2 teaspoons chopped fresh rosemary leaves
a few drops of garlic juice
salt
freshly ground pepper
peanut oil to cook quail
5 tablespoons Calvados
5 tablespoons port
melted clear honey to glaze
canapés:
6 slices French bread
cream for spreading

Dry the quail with paper towels. In a small bowl, mix the butter, herbs, garlic juice, salt and pepper. Put a walnut-sized piece of this flavored butter inside each quail.

Place the quail on a well-oiled baking sheet and place under a preheated very hot broiler. Turn the quail to brown on all sides. Remove the quail.

Warm the Calvados in a saucepan, ignite and carefully pour the Calvados over the quail. Transfer the birds to a large roasting pan. Deglaze the broiling pan with the port, bring the liquid to the boil and pour over the quail. Cover them with foil and set aside until cooking time.

To cook the quail: 45 minutes before serving time, slowly heat the quail in a preheated 300° oven. Remove foil 10 minutes before serving, paint each bird with a little melted honey and return to the oven to give the skin a crisp golden finish.

To make the canapés: arrange the French bread slices on a baking sheet, spread each slice liberally with cream and bake in the oven until crisp.

Serve the quail with a canapé and jardinière de petits pois.

1 cup water
1 teaspoon sugar
salt
freshly ground pepper
1 lb fresh young peas, shelled
¼ lb smoked ham, diced finely
1 onion, chopped finely
1 carrot, chopped finely

Place the water, sugar, salt and pepper in a saucepan and bring to the boil. Add the peas and simmer gently for 5 minutes.

Fry the ham in a small pan until lightly browned. Remove with a slotted spoon and set aside. In the same pan, fry the onion and carrot for a few minutes.

Add the ham, onion and carrot to the saucepan containing the peas. Simmer until tender. Drain and serve.

Below: Cailles à la Normande sur canapé

TARTELETTES
AU COINTREAU

sweet pastry:
6 tablespoons unsalted butter, cut in pieces
2 medium eggs
$\frac{1}{2}$ cup sugar
a pinch of salt
$1\frac{2}{3}$ cups all-purpose flour
orange cream filling:
$\frac{1}{2}$ cup sugar
$\frac{1}{4}$ cup butter, softened
3 medium eggs, beaten
grated rind of $\frac{1}{4}$ lemon
grated rind and juice of $\frac{1}{2}$ orange
juice of $\frac{1}{2}$ lemon
to decorate:
2 tablespoons Cointreau
segments of 2 oranges, all membrane and pith
    removed

To make the sweet pastry: place the butter, eggs, sugar and salt in a food processor and process until well mixed. Add the flour and blend again until the mixture forms a dough. Remove dough from the processor and form into a ball.

If making the pastry by hand, sift the flour into a bowl. Make a well in the center and place the butter, eggs, sugar and salt in the well. Mix the ingredients in the well with your fingertips and gradually mix in the flour until the mixture forms a ball. Do not overwork the pastry. If the dough is too soft add a little flour or, if too dry, add water.

Wrap the dough in plastic wrap or a lightly dampened cloth and refrigerate for at least 1 hour.

To cook the pastry shells: knead the pastry a little before rolling out on a lightly floured board. Cut in 6 squares and place in 6 individual 4-inch tartlet pans. The pastry will hang over the sides a little. Pat pastry gently against base and sides of each pan and trim edges with fingertips. The pastry around the rims of the pans must not be too thin or it will break when unmolding.

Cook pastry shells on a baking sheet in a preheated 400° oven, until rims have browned and pastry is cooked (about 8 minutes). Cool shells a little in pans before turning on to a wire rack.

To prepare the decoration: pour the Cointreau over the orange segments in a small bowl and allow them to macerate.

To make the orange cream filling: place the sugar, softened butter, eggs, rinds and lemon and orange juice in a saucepan. Stir over low heat, whisking constantly, until the mixture thickens. Remove from stove immediately and plunge the bottom of the saucepan in cold water to arrest cooking. Cool to lukewarm.

When the pastry shells are cold, spoon in the filling and smooth tops with a spatula. Chill. Just before serving, arrange 3 drained orange segments on top of each tartelette.

Above: Tartelettes au Cointreau
Above left: Classic Brie with grapes and walnuts

99

CLASSIC ITALIAN
FOR EIGHT

Risotto al Frutti di Mare

Filetti d'Anatra al Burro Rosso
Julienne di Legumi

Insalata Verde e Rossa

Formaggi

Gelato di Fragole

lassical Italian food is really very contemporary because it is simple and tasty. In Italy there is a wealth of dishes but the treatment of ingredients is always straightforward, with a reliance on fresh rather than processed foods. Because Italian food relies on flavor rather than complex methods of preparation, it adapts well to any occasion. In Italian cooking there seems to be no such thing as a dish that is difficult to prepare. The cook is an artisan rather than an artist, although the finished result is undeniably appealing. Basic hearty flavors are complemented by crisp vegetables and salads in a culinary style that is equally appropriate served indoors or out.

This menu for a relaxed, sit-down dinner provides a combination of flavors that complement each other superbly. A meal automatically seems more special if it is organized to a theme. However, even if planning to a theme, do not be afraid to improvise, for example, by adding a touch of tandoori powder to a seafood risotto.

Fillets of duck breast, a quick-cooking main course served with a velvety red wine sauce, are accompanied by crisp julienne vegetables after which a selection of cheeses is served, followed by strawberry ice cream to cleanse and freshen the palate.

Left: Filetti d'anatra al burro rosso (page 102)

RISOTTO AL FRUTTI DE MARE
(Seafood Risotto)

¼ cup butter
4 green onions, chopped finely
1 piece fresh ginger, about 1¼ inches long,
  peeled and chopped finely
1 medium-size carrot, peeled and chopped
  finely
1 stalk celery, chopped finely
1 lb imported Italian rice (Arborio)
1 glass dry white wine
4 cups chicken stock (good quality stock cubes
  can be used)
1 pinch saffron, diluted in a little warm water
2 heaping teaspoons tandoori powder
3 lb raw shrimps, peeled and deveined
1½ lb scallops
2 to 3 dozen opened oysters, liquid reserved
4 tablespoons cream
scant 1 cup finely grated imported Parmesan
  cheese
salt
freshly ground pepper
a few unpeeled cooked shrimps to garnish

Melt the butter in a large frying pan.
Add the green onions, ginger, carrot and
celery and sauté for a few minutes until
translucent. Add the rice, wine, some
stock and, stirring constantly, cook until
the rice has absorbed the fluid.

Add the saffron, tandoori powder, liquid from the oysters and more stock.
Continue to cook, covered, stirring occasionally until the rice is nearly cooked.
Add the shrimps and scallops; mix carefully and cook until the shrimps are pink
and the scallops are translucent. Add the
oysters and toss around to heat through.
(Do not overcook seafood or it will
toughen and shrink.)

When the rice is "al dente", remove
from the stove, add the cream and Parmesan cheese. Taste for salt and pepper
and leave to rest for a few minutes before
transferring to a warmed serving platter.
Serve immediately, garnished with a few
unpeeled cooked shrimps.
Note: The quantity of stock needed for
the risotto will depend on the quality of
the rice and degree of cooking.

FILETTI D'ANATRA AL BURRO ROSSO
(Duck Fillets with Red Butter Sauce)

red butter sauce:
8 shallots, chopped finely
1½ cups red wine
scant 1 cup cream
1¼ cups butter, cut in small pieces
salt
freshly ground pepper

duck breasts:
8 duck breasts, skin left on
salt
freshly ground pepper
½ cup red wine

To make the red butter sauce: place the
shallots in a small saucepan with the

wine and reduce over low heat until there
are about 2 tablespoons of liquid left.
Add the cream and reduce again, until
the sauce coats the back of a spoon and
looks syrupy. Remove the saucepan from
the heat and add the butter a piece at a
time, beating well after the addition of
each piece. Taste for salt and pepper and
set the sauce aside in a warm place.
To cook the duck: brown the fillets of duck
in a heavy saucepan, skin side first without adding extra fat. Spoon off the fat

which is rendered and turn the breasts to cook the other side (the flesh should remain pink). Add salt and pepper to taste and arrange on a warm serving plate. Remove any fat from the saucepan, add the wine and deglaze the pan by incorporating all the particles left in the pan. Whisk the juices into the red butter sauce. Spoon a little of the sauce over the fillets and serve the rest separately in a sauce boat.

JULIENNE DI LEGUMI
(Vegetables Julienne)

½ lb very young green beans, trimmed
½ lb carrots, peeled
1 yellow or red sweet pepper, seeded and
    quartered
6 shallots, peeled
1 piece of fresh ginger, about 3 inches long,
    peeled
¼ cup butter
salt
freshly ground pepper

Cut the vegetables and the ginger into fine julienne (matchstick) strips.

Melt the butter in a large frying pan, add the vegetables, salt and pepper to taste, cover and steam gently for about 2 minutes, until the vegetables are cooked but still crisp.

INSALATA VERDE E ROSSA
(Red and Green Salad)

1 head romaine or other lettuce
1 radicchio
Marc's vinaigrette:
scant ½ cup white wine vinegar
1 tablespoon lemon juice
⅘ cup extra virgin olive oil
scant ¼ cup grape seed oil
1 teaspoon Dijon mustard
1 teaspoon sugar
salt
freshly ground pepper

Rinse and thoroughly dry the salad leaves. Transfer to a salad bowl.
To make the vinaigrette: mix all the ingredients in a screw-top jar and shake to combine. Dress the salad just before serving.

Left: Risotto al frutti di mare
Right: Gelato di fragole

GELATO DI FRAGOLE
(Strawberry Ice Cream)

4 egg yolks
1 cup sugar
1 pint fresh strawberries or 2 9-oz packages
    frozen strawberries, puréed
1½ cups cream, whipped
1 cup of strawberries for decoration

Using a whisk or an electric mixer, beat together the egg yolks and sugar until thick and creamy and the mixture forms "ribbons" (when the whisk is lifted, a trail will remain on the surface).

Carefully fold the egg mixture and the puréed fruit into the whipped cream. When thoroughly combined pour the mixture into an ice-cream machine. Freeze until almost firm, then transfer the mixture to a mold. Cover and freeze until required.
To serve: unmold the ice cream on to a pretty serving dish and decorate with fresh strawberries.

Platter of Smoked Fish with Watercress Mayonnaise and
Coral Mayonnaise
Pita Bread

Sweetbreads à la Carte
Nests of Wild Rice

Chocolate Hearts with Coffee Anglaise and Crème Anglaise

Violet-topped Chocolates
Coffee

TEENAGE DINNER
FOR EIGHT

A formal black tie dinner party is a delightful treat to lay on for teenagers. This sophisticated menu is designed to encourage young people to experience new tastes. Young adults appreciate well-presented food and often revel in the formality of an adult-style occasion.

Here is a light, well-coordinated menu, in keeping with the current trend away from heavy food. The results are stunning, but preparation time is not excessive – a factor that will be particularly welcome if the dishes are to be prepared by a busy parent.

A delicious platter of smoked fish, including oysters, mussels, stuffed squid, pink trout and salmon, is served to start. Sweetbreads, which many would consider an acquired taste, are topped with a flavorsome sorrel sauce and accompanied by lightly-cooked spinach and nests of wild rice filled with tiny colorful balls of pumpkin, potato and chayote.

If romance is in the air, the youngsters will appreciate a chocolate heart, made either as one gâteau or in individual molds and served with crème anglaise and coffee anglaise. The chocolate hearts can be prepared the day before and refrigerated. The sauces actually gain flavor if left to stand overnight.

Serve fine violet-adorned chocolates with the coffee. They are simple to make and are the perfect finale to the dinner.

Left: Chocolate hearts with coffee Anglaise and Crème Anglaise

PLATTER OF SMOKED FISH

a variety of smoked fish: oysters, mussels,
    stuffed squid, trout and salmon
garden cress or watercress
basic mayonnaise:
6 egg yolks
2 tablespoons water
2 cups safflower oil
2 tablespoons lemon juice
coral mayonnaise:
the coral from 12 scallops or 1 sweet red
    pepper, seeded
watercress mayonnaise:
bunch of watercress

Arrange the smoked fish on individual plates or on one large platter and garnish with garden cress or watercress.

Put the egg yolks and water in a blender or food processor and blend for 6 seconds. While the machine is running, slowly add 1 cup of safflower oil. When the mixture is thick, add 1 tablespoon of lemon juice. Blend again and gradually add another cup of oil. Add remaining lemon juice when mixture has thickened. Divide this quantity into 2 bowls.

To make the coral mayonnaise: purée the coral from the scallops in a blender or food processor and add to one half of the mayonnaise. If coral is unobtainable chop and purée the red pepper.

To make the watercress mayonnaise: take the leaves of watercress and blanch in boiling salted water for a few seconds. Drain and dry thoroughly. Place in a blender or food processor with remaining mayonnaise and blend until thoroughly mixed.

To serve: transfer the mayonnaises to two serving bowls and pass around with the seafood platter and hot pita bread.

Left: Platter of smoked fish

105

PITA BREAD

The flavor of pita bread can be improved with little effort. You will need one package of pita bread.

Split each pita bread in two. Cut the thin pita halves in pieces and butter each piece on both sides. Sprinkle generously with lemon pepper and fennel seed.

Place on a baking sheet and cook in a preheated 350° oven until browned on one side. Turn the bread over and cook for an additional few minutes on the second side.

SWEETBREADS À LA CARTE

1¾ lb fresh sweetbreads
2 quarts cold water
3 teaspoons butter
1 large carrot, sliced finely
1 small onion, chopped finely
2 shallots, sliced finely
1 clove garlic, crushed
1 sprig of thyme
1 bay leaf
salt
freshly ground pepper
sauce:
½ cup vermouth (preferably Noilly Prat)
1 cup cream
2 tablespoons coarsely chopped sorrel
6 tablespoons butter
6 oz fresh young spinach

To prepare the sweetbreads: rinse the sweetbreads under cold running water for 5 to 10 minutes. Put the sweetbreads in a saucepan with the cold water, bring to the boil and boil for 3 minutes. Immediately refresh under cold running water. Drain, remove the membranes and cut away any fibrous pieces. Wrap the sweetbreads in a clean dish towel and put them under a weighted board in the refrigerator, overnight, to expel any water and to give them a flat shape.

To cook the sweetbreads: melt the butter in a flameproof casserole and sprinkle in the carrot, onion and shallots. Lay the sweetbreads on top. Season with garlic, thyme, bay leaf, salt and pepper. Cover and cook in a preheated 325° oven for 35 to 45 minutes.

Remove sweetbreads and keep warm between two plates in a low oven with the door slightly open.

To make the sauce: add the vermouth to the casserole and cook steadily until reduced a little. Add the cream, bring to the boil and add the sorrel. Cook for 1–2 minutes.

Just before serving, add 4 tablespoons butter to the sauce, a small piece at a time, stirring constantly until the sauce is thick and creamy. Season to taste.

To assemble: melt the remaining butter in a clean pan, add the spinach and cook over gentle heat until soft. Add salt and pepper to taste.

Cut the sweetbreads into even slices. Purée the sauce in a blender or food processor until smooth.

Place a mound of spinach on each plate, scatter sweetbreads on top and spoon a little of the sauce over the sweetbreads. Serve immediately with the wild rice nests.

NESTS OF WILD RICE

The chayote is a delicious vegetable, little known outside the United States and its native Mexico. It is a pale-green, pear-shaped member of the gourd family, and is at its best when only a few days old. When cut, chayote exudes a liquid that can stain the hands, so always peel it under water or preferably cook without removing the skins.

wild rice:
4 tablespoons butter
2 tablespoons finely diced carrot
2 tablespoons finely diced celery
2 tablespoons finely chopped green onion
1 cup wild rice
1½ cups chicken stock
vegetables:
2 chayotes
¼ lb pumpkin
1 large potato
2 tablespoons chopped fresh parsley

To cook the wild rice: melt half the butter in a saucepan. Add the carrot, celery and green onion, cover the pan and cook over low heat for 10 minutes until the vegetables are soft, but not brown. Stir in the rice and cook for 2 to 3 minutes, coating the rice with butter.

Bring the stock to the boil in a separate saucepan and pour over the rice. Bring to the boil again, cover tightly and lower the heat. Cook for 30 minutes or until the rice is tender and has absorbed all the liquid.

To prepare the vegetables: peel the chayotes under running water and remove the center cores. With a melon baller, shape the chayote flesh into small balls. Peel and shape the pumpkin and potato in the same way.

Bring a pan of salted water to the boil, add the pumpkin, potato and chayote balls and cook until just tender. Immediately drain the balls and plunge them into iced water to arrest cooking. Drain and set aside.

Melt 1 tablespoon of the remaining butter in a frying pan, add the parsley and cook over moderate heat for 2 minutes. Stir into the rice and toss well.

Mold the rice into the shape of 8 nests. Arrange the nests on a platter and keep warm. Melt the remaining 1 tablespoon of butter in a frying pan over moderate heat, add the reserved pumpkin, chayote and potato balls and heat them through swiftly. Fill the wild rice nests and serve immediately.

Left: Sweetbreads à la carte with nests of wild rice

CHOCOLATE HEARTS

2 oz semisweet chocolate
1¼ cups milk
½ cup sifted cocoa
¼ cup butter
⅔ cup sugar
3 egg yolks
1 envelope gelatin
¼ cup water
1¼ cups heavy cream

Melt the chocolate in the top of a double boiler set over simmering water. Allow to cool. Put milk, sifted cocoa, butter and sugar in a saucepan and bring to the boil. In a bowl, beat the egg yolks until creamy and mix with the melted chocolate. Strain on the hot milk mixture and whisk well.

In a small bowl soften the gelatin in the water and add to the chocolate custard mixture. Stir well to make sure the gelatin is completely dissolved. In a large bowl, whip the cream to soft peaks. Fold in the cold chocolate mixture with a metal spoon. Pour into 8 small heart-shaped molds and refrigerate overnight. *To serve:* unmold each chocolate heart on to a chilled dessert plate. Spoon a little crème anglaise on one side of each heart and a little coffee anglaise on the other.

CRÈME ANGLAISE

1 vanilla bean
1½ cups milk
4 egg yolks
3 tablespoons sugar

Split the vanilla bean in half lengthwise and put it in a heavy-bottomed saucepan with the milk. Slowly bring to the boil, turn off the heat and leave to infuse the flavor.

Break up the yolks with a whisk, add the sugar and beat until smooth. Pour the hot, vanilla-flavored milk over the egg mixture and strain into a saucepan. Discard vanilla bean. Cook the custard, stirring constantly, until it coats the back of the spoon. Allow to cool, stirring from time to time to prevent a skin forming. Cover and refrigerate until serving time.

Above: Coffee served with violet-topped chocolates

COFFEE ANGLAISE

1 cup milk
3 tablespoons sugar
2 teaspoons instant coffee powder
3 egg yolks

Put the milk in a heavy-bottomed saucepan with 2 tablespoons sugar and the instant coffee powder. Bring to the boil, turn off the heat and stir until the coffee has dissolved.

In a large bowl, beat the egg yolks with the rest of the sugar until white and fluffy. Pour on the hot coffee-milk, stirring well. Return the mixture to the saucepan, place over low heat and cook, stirring all the time, until the custard coats the back of the spoon. Remove from the stove and strain into a bowl. Cover the surface of the coffee anglaise with plastic wrap, cool and refrigerate. *Note:* This can be made the day before serving.

VIOLET-TOPPED CHOCOLATES

1 cup pitted dates, chopped
1 tablespoon mixed peel
½ cup preserved ginger, drained and chopped
6 tablespoons butter
¼ cup raw sugar
3 cups muesli flakes
to decorate:
8 oz semisweet chocolate, melted
crystallized violets

Place all the ingredients except the chocolate and violets in a heavy-bottomed saucepan and heat gently until the butter has melted. Stir to mix well. Do not allow the mixture to boil. Press the mixture into a buttered jelly-roll pan and set aside to cool. When cold and firm, cut with tiny molds or roll in little balls.
To decorate: cover with melted chocolate and top each with a crystallized violet.

107

Radishes with Mustard Seed Mayonnaise
Crusty Bread

Poached Boned Chicken with Cardamom Bread Sauce

Weed Salad

Berry Fruits with Clotted Cream and Sugar Bark

Turkish Delight
Coffee

SUMMER DINNER
FOR FOUR

T he fields and the garden are useful resources to tap when planning an interesting meal. Many so-called weeds, such as dandelions, rocket, purslane and baby milkweed thistles, can be eaten in salads, combined perhaps with tender young spinach leaves. In this menu a weed salad is used to mop up the juices of delicately spiced chicken served with cardamom-flavored bread sauce. Grapes and sweet-potato sticks are complementary accompaniments.

This meal can be prepared fairly quickly, although some steps can be made ahead to save time. What could be simpler or more delicious than crunchy fresh radishes served with crusty white bread, plenty of coarse salt and a tangy mustard seed mayonnaise?

With even the most basic ingredients food can look striking. The crunchy sugar bark that is used to adorn bowls of fresh berries and clotted cream is a good example. If necessary this can be made the day before and kept crisp in an airtight tin.

Left: The perfect finale – coffee served with Turkish delight

RADISHES WITH MUSTARD SEED MAYONNAISE

2 bunches fresh radishes, washed and trimmed
½ loaf white crusty bread, in chunks
coarse salt
mustard seed mayonnaise:
½ cup olive oil
½ cup vegetable oil
1 teaspoon mustard seeds
2 egg yolks
freshly ground pepper
juice of ½ lemon

Wash the radishes under cold water and pull away the outer leaves. Serve with chunks of crusty bread, plenty of coarse salt and the mayonnaise.
To make the mayonnaise: combine the oils in a cup and heat the mustard seeds in 1 tablespoon of the oil until they burst.

Return the cooking oil to the oil in the cup. Allow the mustard seeds to cool a little.

Prepare the mayonnaise in a bowl, using a wooden spoon or, preferably, in a warm mortar and pestle. Place the egg yolks in the bowl or mortar and add the oil, drop by drop, beating vigorously. Add the oil in larger quantities as the sauce thickens. The mayonnaise should stand in stiff peaks. Add pepper to taste. Heat the lemon juice in a small saucepan. When it begins to boil whisk it into the mayonnaise together with the mustard seeds.

Left: Radishes with mustard seed mayonnaise

109

POACHED BONED CHICKEN

chicken:
2 small chickens
1¼ cups hot water
salt
freshly ground pepper
garnish:
1½ cups large white grapes
a little dry white wine
1 medium sweet potato

1¼ cups water
2 teaspoons butter

To prepare the grapes: blanch the grapes in boiling water for 10 seconds, then refresh in ice cold water. Cut in half lengthwise, seed and peel. Macerate the grapes for 1 hour in white wine.

To cook the chickens: cut each chicken in half through the breast bone. Push the flesh away from the carcass with your fingers. Sever all the ball joints of leg and wing and strip the flesh back along the bone towards the tips. A small sharp knife is required to sever tendons as you work back. You may leave the wing tip either as it is or discard it altogether, as it is impossible to bone. Reserve the carcass and leg and wing bones.

Trim the excess fat from the flesh. Wrap the boned leg, thigh and wing sections around each breast in a shape loosely resembling a sausage. Tie into shape with kitchen string and place in a roasting pan on top of the flattened carcasses and bones. Cover with the hot but not boiling water, salt and pepper. Cover the pan with foil, sealing the edges, and place in a preheated 400° oven for 35 minutes, after which the chicken should be moist, tender and ready to serve.

To cook the sweet potato: slice the potato into julienne strips twice the thickness of matchsticks. Place 2 cups of julienne into 1¼ cups water. Add the butter, and bring to the boil, reduce the heat and simmer for 10 minutes. Drain.

To serve: place the poached chicken portions on a platter and garnish with the drained grapes and sweet potato julienne.

CARDAMOM BREAD SAUCE

1 small white onion, sliced
1 cup milk
3 cloves
3 cardamom pods
1½ cups fine white bread crumbs
salt
freshly ground pepper
1 walnut-sized piece of butter
2 teaspoons cream
cayenne pepper or chili flakes

Place the onion, milk, cloves and cardamom pods in a double boiler and bring slowly to simmer. (It should take at least ½ an hour to infuse the milk with flavor.) Remove the onion and spices and stir in the bread crumbs. Season with salt and pepper and continue cooking for another 10 to 15 minutes. The sauce should be thick enough to spread slightly when spooned on to a plate. The consistency of the sauce can be adjusted by adding more milk or bread crumbs.

Before serving, stir in ½ the butter and the cream, pour into a warm tureen or boat, garnish with the remaining butter, cayenne or a few chili flakes.

Left: Poached boned chicken served with cardamom bread sauce

WEED SALAD

When picking the weeds for the salad, be sure to consult an expert as not all wild plants are as innocent as those mentioned below. The weed salad should be fairly bitter to contrast with the delicate subtlety of the main dish. It should not be served on side plates but should be used to mop up the lingering traces of chicken juices and bread sauce.

mustard (Sisymbrium officinale)
milkweed thistle (Sonchus oleraceus)
purslane (Portulaca oleracea)
dandelion (Taraxacum officinale)
(*if any weeds are unavailable, substitute curly endive*)
tender young leaves from heart of young

spinach plants
walnut oil or olive oil
vinegar
salt
freshly ground pepper

Rinse and drain all weeds and spinach twice; the total combined weight of the weeds should equal the weight of the spinach, and all should fill ¾ of a standard domestic colander.

Lay out weeds and spinach on a flat platter and dress first with walnut oil. Then trickle vinegar over and finally season with salt and freshly ground pepper. Do not amalgamate oil and vinegar before dressing the salad.

Above: Weed salad
Below: Berry fruits with clotted cream and sugar bark

BERRY FRUITS WITH CLOTTED CREAM AND SUGAR BARK

1¼ *cups heavy cream*
1 *vanilla bean*
2 *cups chilled berry fruits*
sugar bark:
½ *cup raw sugar*
½ *cup granulated sugar*
1 *tablespoon coffee sugar crystals*

To make the sugar bark: this should be made the day before using. Lightly grease 2 pieces of foil which will fit in your broiler pan. Turn the foil up slightly at the edges to prevent spillage. Sprinkle a light covering of sugars over foil and scatter a few coffee crystals on the sugar. Place under a preheated hot broiler and check every 10 seconds. The sugar will melt into a thin sheet and some caramelization will occur. This happens quickly and requires full concentration to prevent burning. As soon as the sugar melts, remove foil sheets from the grill and allow to cool. The resulting "bark" comes off the foil easily and can be kept for several days in an airtight tin until you wish to use it.

To make the clotted cream: place the cream and vanilla bean in a small saucepan over moderate heat and bring to just below boiling point. Remove from heat, discard the bean and divide the cream among 6 glass coupes. Allow to cool and refrigerate.

Just before serving, tumble berry fruits on top of the set cream and decorate each dessert with shards of sugar bark for a spectacular effect.

111

Salad of Squab with Fresh Figs

**Cornets of Trout with Squash Flowers, Tomato and Chervil
Beurre Blanc**

Veal Cutlets in Crépinette

Poached Tamarillos with Coconut Junket

GOURMET DINNER
FOR FOUR

A stretch of the imagination: four small courses delicately balanced by the lightest conceivable sauces, designed to be laid out with artistic flair. The influences of the greatest exponents of nouvelle cuisine are evident in this dinner menu. Helpings are dainty, sauces pre-eminent, decoration striking but simple. Fresh fruit is used to enhance the gamy taste of a squab salad, with subsidiary flavorings of roasted pine nuts, cooked beets, croutons and carrot sticks. The salad is served on a film of jellied consommé.

A course guaranteed to melt in the mouth follows. Fillets of trout are rolled into a cornet shapes and filled with delectable prawn mousse, which is also piped into accompanying squash flowers. This dish has to be served immediately after poaching. Veal cutlets, normally a mundane dish, are enlivened by the addition of a savory stuffing and a vegetable garnish.

After such a rich main course a light fresh dessert is required; we suggest poached tamarillos with a refreshing coconut junket – a childhood food revitalized.

Left: Elegant salad of squab with fresh figs

SALAD OF SQUAB WITH FRESH FIGS

2 1-lb squabs
a little butter to roast squabs
croutons:
2 slices bread, cut in small cubes
butter or oil for frying
jellied consommé:
1¾ cups game consommé
1½ teaspoons gelatin
salad:
1 tablespoon roasted pine nuts
1 large cooked beet, peeled and cubed
1 small carrot, julienned
a little olive oil
a little balsamic vinegar
salt
freshly ground pepper
4 fresh figs, peeled and quartered

Roast the squabs with a little butter in a preheated 400° oven for 15 to 20 minutes.

Set aside to cool.
To make the croutons: melt the butter or oil in a frying pan, add the croutons and toss in the hot fat until brown and crisp. Set aside.
To make the jellied consommé: place the consommé in a pan and heat until simmering. Meanwhile, soak the gelatin in a little cold water for 5 minutes, then add to the simmering consommé. Cool and pour into 4 shallow soup bowls. Leave in a cool place to set.
To make the salad: bone the squabs and slice the meat. Toss the squab meat in a bowl with the pine nuts, beets, carrot, oil and vinegar and salt and pepper to taste. Arrange the salad and quarters of figs on the set consommé in the individual dishes. Sprinkle the salad with the croutons and serve.

CORNETS OF TROUT WITH CHERVIL BEURRE BLANC

1 lb green shrimps, peeled and cleaned
2 egg whites
1¼ cups heavy cream
salt
freshly ground pepper
2 trout, filleted, skinned and boned
8 baby squash with flowers attached
chervil beurre blanc:
3 tablespoons white wine vinegar
3 tablespoons water
3 tablespoons finely chopped shallots
salt
freshly ground pepper
2 tablespoons crème fraîche or cream
½ cup soft unsalted butter
1 large ripe tomato, peeled, seeded and cut in small dice

1 small bunch of chervil, leaves chopped roughly

Place the shrimps in a blender or food processor with the egg whites and cream and process until thick and creamy. Be careful not to overblend or the cream will separate. Add salt and pepper to taste. Pass the mixture through a fine sieve or mouli and place in a pastry bag fitted with a large, star-shaped tube.

Roll the trout fillets into cone shapes and pipe some of the shrimp mousse into each. Fill the squash flowers carefully with the mousse. Place the squash flowers and cornets of trout in a steamer and set aside.

To make the chervil beurre blanc: place the vinegar, water, shallots and salt and pepper to taste in a small stainless steel saucepan and boil over low heat until reduced to 1 tablespoon. Add the cream and beat in the butter, small pieces at a time. Strain the mixture and keep warm.
To cook the trout and squash: steam over hot stock for about 10 minutes (depending on size).
To serve: add the tomato and chervil to the beurre blanc. Place one cornet of trout on a warm serving plate and spoon the sauce over the base of the cornet. Arrange two squash on each plate and serve immediately.

Above: Cornet of trout with chervil beurre blanc

114

VEAL CUTLETS IN CRÉPINETTE

4 ½-lb veal cutlets, trimmed
butter
3 slices bacon
4 shallots or green onions
1 clove garlic
¼ lb button mushrooms
1 teaspoon fresh thyme
salt
freshly ground pepper
enough pork caul to cover the cutlets
vegetable garnish:
12 small green onions
12 turned carrots
⅔ cup very strong veal stock or veal glacé
2 oz bone marrow, very thinly sliced

To prepare the cutlets: heat a large frying pan, add the veal cutlets and brown quickly in a little butter on both sides. Cool on a wire rack.
To make the filling: sauté the bacon in the pan, with the shallots, garlic, mushrooms and thyme until the liquid has evaporated. Allow the mixture to get cold. Place in a food processor with salt and pepper and process about 1 or 2 minutes.
To prepare cutlets for cooking: place ¼ of the filling across back of each cutlet and wrap in a pork caul. Wrap once or twice around and place on a buttered tray.
To cook the cutlets: bake in a preheated 425° oven for about 20 to 25 minutes, depending on how you like your meat (rare, medium or well done). When the cutlets are cooked, rest them in a warm place for 10 minutes.
To make the vegetable garnish: boil the onions and carrots for a few minutes in salted water. Drain. Pour strong veal stock, or veal glacé, into a small pan and toss the vegetables for a few seconds to heat through. Poach the pieces of bone marrow in boiling, salted water, just before serving.
To serve: slice each cutlet into three, leaving bone in one piece, and spoon over some sauce, vegetables and a few pieces of marrow.

POACHED TAMARILLOS WITH COCONUT JUNKET

4 tamarillos
1½ cups sugar
1½ cups water
coconut junket:
1 quart milk
1 cup shredded coconut
2 junket tablets
2 tablespoons cold water
2 tablespoons shredded coconut to decorate

To cook the tamarillos: leave the stems on the tamarillos and cut a small cross at the other end with a small knife.

Heat the sugar and water, stirring until the sugar has dissolved. Bring to the boil and drop in tamarillos. Cover and simmer very slowly until the tamarillo skins can be removed easily. Peel tamarillos then leave them in the syrup until you are ready to serve. Drain before serving.
To make the coconut junket: bring the milk and shredded coconut to simmering point (do not boil). Allow to cool to lukewarm. Strain and squeeze the coconut well to extract flavor. Discard coconut. Dissolve the junket tablets in the cold water and pour into the milk. Pour quickly into individual bowls and leave to stand, undisturbed, for 20 minutes.
To prepare the decoration: place the coconut on a baking sheet and bake in a preheated 350° oven until golden brown. Cool and sprinkle over the junket before serving.

Top: Veal cutlets in crépinette
Above: Poached tamarillo with coconut junket

115

FORMAL DINNER
—FOR EIGHT—

Cold Tomato and Basil Soup

Mussels Oscar

Stuffed Guinea Fowl with Bacon Rolls and Bread Sauce

Fava Bean and Asparagus Medley

Fresh Peaches with Apricot Ice Cream

or

Apricot Bavarois with Peach-Leaf Sauce

T his is a menu for a special dinner with a strong emphasis on visual appeal. There are four courses, but none is too substantial. The meal begins with a refreshing chilled tomato soup, which is garnished with slivers of ham and finely shredded fresh basil.

Ginger and cucumber are the unusual flavors that supplement, but do not dominate, the taste of mussels Oscar. The mussels are simmered in white wine and then enriched with cream and the buttery vegetables. Stuffed guinea fowl follows, served flanked with broiled rolls of bacon, old-fashioned gravy and bread sauce and a medley of fava beans and asparagus that can be cooked ahead, and then tossed in hot, melted butter just before serving.

A choice of desserts adds a touch of style to a meal. The selection: apricot bavarois with a sauce made of egg yolks and an infusion of peach leaves, or fresh peaches topped with apricot ice cream, and garnished with amaretti cookies. Both are palate-cleansing finales.

COLD TOMATO AND BASIL SOUP

12 large ripe red tomatoes, chopped roughly
1 teaspoon grated onion
salt
freshly ground pepper
a good pinch of sugar
1 teaspoon finely grated lemon rind
juice of 1 lemon
1¼ cups cream
garnish:
8 tablespoons finely cut ham strips
8 tablespoons whipped cream
finely shredded basil

Purée the tomatoes in a blender or food processor with the onion, salt, pepper, sugar, lemon rind and juice. Strain, pressing down well with a wooden spoon to extract all the juices. Add the cream and season to taste. Pour into a container, cover and chill. Chill 8 soup bowls.

To serve: place 1 tablespoon ham strips in each chilled soup bowl. Pour in the soup and top each portion with 1 tablespoon whipped cream. Sprinkle with freshly shredded basil. (*Pictured left.*)

STUFFED GUINEA FOWL WITH BACON ROLLS

8 guinea fowl
salt
freshly ground pepper
18 bacon slices
soft butter
herb stuffing:
¾ cup plus 2 tablespoons butter
2 onions, chopped finely
1 1-lb loaf bread made into bread crumbs
⅔ cup chopped fresh parsley
1 tablespoon chopped mixed fresh herbs
salt
freshly ground pepper
old-fashioned gravy:
wing tips, necks of fowls
1 onion, peeled and quartered
1 celery stalk, chopped roughly
1 carrot, peeled and cut in large chunks
1 bay leaf
few sprigs fresh herbs including parsley stems
6 cups water
1 cup white wine
1½ tablespoons flour
salt
freshly ground pepper
garnish:
16 slices bacon

To cook the guinea fowl: remove the necks and any remaining feathers from the guinea fowl and cut off the wing tips (reserve necks, wing tips or any giblets for the stock to make gravy). Wash and dry fowls with paper towels and set aside.
To make the stuffing: melt the butter in a large frying pan, add the chopped onions and cook over gentle heat until the onions have softened a little. Remove the pan from the heat, add the bread crumbs, parsley, herbs, salt and pepper.

Mix well. Stuff the stomach cavities of the birds and secure neck and cavity openings with poultry pins.

Liberally butter a large roasting pan. Butter each bird and sprinkle with a little salt and plenty of freshly ground pepper. Arrange the birds in the roasting pan. Cut each bacon slice in 3 pieces and drape over each bird. Bake the stuffed guinea fowl on the center shelf of a preheated 375° oven for 1 hour, basting frequently.
To make the bacon roll garnish: roll bacon into neat rolls and thread on a skewer. When the guinea fowl are cooked, quickly cook the rolls under a hot broiler, turning once. Serve one or two per person.
To make the stock for the gravy: place the reserved wing tips and guinea fowl necks in a large saucepan with the vegetables, herbs, water and wine. Bring to the boil, then lower the heat and simmer until required.

When the guinea fowl are cooked, transfer them to a heated platter and keep them warm in the oven while you make the gravy.

Pour off all but 1 tablespoon of fat from the roasting pan and place the pan over moderate heat. Sprinkle in the 1½ table-spoons flour and mix well, scraping pan to remove any brown bits of meat sediment to help color the gravy. Pour in a little of the stock and mix to dissolve all the flour lumps. Pour in more stock, whisking constantly until the gravy bubbles and has the required thickness. Add salt and pepper to taste. Strain into a warm gravy boat.

MUSSELS OSCAR

7 lb mussels
white wine to open mussels
sauce:
½ the juice from mussels (after opening)
½ cup white wine
1 cup cream
1 cup unsalted butter, cut in small cubes
finely ground pepper
¾ cup fine strips fresh ginger
¾ cup fine strips cucumber

To open the mussels: wash and clean the mussels and pull beards. Discard any that are already open. Cover the bottom of a large pan or deep-frying pan with about ½ inch white wine. Bring to the boil and put in a few mussels. After a few seconds, the mussels will open. Remove from the pan and cut the mussels away from their shells. Put the mussels, with juices from the shells, in a bowl while you open the remainder. Cook only a few at a time so the mussels do not overcook and toughen.
To make the sauce: when all the mussels are cooked, strain off the juice and put half in a saucepan with the white wine. Boil over high heat to reduce. Add the cream and continue to boil rapidly until reduced to about ¾ cup.

Lower heat and beat in pieces of butter, a few at a time, until the sauce thickens. Taste for pepper. Add the mussels, ginger and cucumber. Quickly heat through. Do not boil or the sauce will separate and the mussels toughen. Spoon on to heated plates and serve at once.

Above: Mussels Oscar

BREAD SAUCE

6 cloves1 small onion, peeled
1 bay leaf
pinch grated nutmeg
2 cups milk
1 cup fresh white bread crumbs
salt
freshly ground pepper
2 tablespoons butter

Stick the cloves into the onion and put in a heavy-bottomed saucepan with the bay leaf, nutmeg, milk, bread crumbs, salt, pepper and butter. Mix the bread crumbs into the milk and butter. Cook over a very low heat, stirring frequently, until the flavor is extracted from the onion and cloves and the sauce thickens. Remove the onion, cloves and bay leaf and transfer to a heated sauce boat. Serve hot with the guinea fowl.

Below: Stuffed guinea fowl with bacon rolls

FAVA BEAN AND ASPARAGUS MEDLEY

4 lb fava beans, shelled
3 bunches asparagus
½ cup butter, more if necessary
salt
freshly ground pepper

Cook the fava beans in a large pan of boiling salted water for 3 to 4 minutes. Drain, slip the beans out of their skins (optional) and immediately refresh under cold water to arrest cooking and set color. Drain again and set aside.

Cut asparagus into bite-sized lengths, discarding hard ends. Cook in same way as the fava beans, and set aside to drain.

Just before serving melt the butter in a large frying pan. Add the fava beans and asparagus and toss quickly with salt and pepper to taste until the vegetables are hot. Add more butter if necessary. Do not overcook or vegetables will lose their color. Serve immediately.

FRESH PEACHES WITH APRICOT ICE CREAM

4 large fresh ripe peaches
apricot ice cream:
2 cups cream
4 egg yolks
1 cup sugar
2 cups apricot purée
2 tablespoons lemon juice
2 tablespoons apricot liqueur
Amaretti cookies to decorate

To make the ice cream: place the cream in a saucepan and bring to the boil. Beat the egg yolks in a bowl with the sugar until light in color. Pour in a little of the boiling cream, mix well and return to the saucepan. Lower the heat and cook, stirring constantly, until the mixture coats the back of a spoon. Allow to cool.

Stir in apricot purée, lemon juice and liqueur. Freeze, using an icecream machine if possible.

Just before serving, halve and pit the peaches and peel the halves. Place a peach half on each serving plate and spoon some apricot ice cream on top. Serve with Amaretti cookies.

APRICOT BAVAROIS WITH PEACH-LEAF SAUCE

1 cup milk
4 egg yolks
1 cup sugar
2½ cups poached apricot purée (including skin)
1 envelope gelatin
water to soften gelatin
vanilla
1¼ cups cream, whipped
peach-leaf sauce:
1½ cups milk
3 or 4 peach leaves or a few drops almond extract
4 egg yolks
¼ cup sugar
garnish:
flaked almonds, toasted

To make the bavarois: bring the milk to the boil. Beat together the egg yolks and sugar. Pour a little milk into the yolk mixture, mix well and return to the saucepan with the apricot purée. Cook over a low heat, stirring all the time, until the mixture coats the back of the spoon. Soften the gelatin in a little cold water. Add to the saucepan and mix well. Stir in a few drops of vanilla and pour into a bowl. Cover and cool. Fold in the whipped cream. Pour into a serving bowl and refrigerate overnight.

To make the sauce: bring the milk and peach leaves to the boil. Allow to infuse so the almond flavor is extracted from the peach leaves. Strain and discard the peach leaves.

Beat the egg yolks with the sugar. Heat the milk to boiling point and pour a little into the egg mixture. Mix well and return to the milk in pan. Cook over a low heat, stirring all the time. until the mixture coats the back of a spoon. Pour into a container, cover and chill overnight in the refrigerator.

To serve: put some of the sauce on a serving plate and spoon a portion of bavarois on top. Scatter toasted almonds over the bavarois and sauce and decorate with a peach leaf.

Left: Fresh peaches with apricot ice cream

MORE TASTE THAN TIME

Of all the fresh and wonderful ingredients available to us, one commodity grows more scarce in direct relation to how busy our lives become. That magic ingredient is time.

While it is true that any social event, however simple, requires quite a lot of hostly effort, there are short cuts that don't have to jeopardize the quality of the food or its presentation.

One of the tricks is to structure your menu around one or two dishes that may be prepared ahead of time. Another is to know, foster and reward your suppliers, especially those that stay open late or are happy to deliver to the kitchen door. A well-stocked emergency shelf can be the source of last-minute inspiration and, at those moments, you'll bless the day you grew fresh herbs on the windowsill or in the garden.

What is of major importance is to recognize the value of the season's yield: what could be more perfect to the eye and the palate than baby radishes served with sweet butter and rough sea salt?

Antipasto

Lamb Fillets with Fresh Rosemary
Spinach Milanese-style

Stuffed Figs

Cheese Board

INTIMATE LUNCH
—————— FOR TWO ——————

Elegance does not always need to be labored over. This simple lunch for two can be prepared quickly, even, if necessary, in the middle of a working day. Inspired by the finest Italian ingredients, this menu is distinguished by a clever combination of the finest fresh ingredients with items from the emergency shelf.

If preparing a meal at the last moment, an informal first course is practical. A hearty platter of antipasto stimulates the appetite and is welcome for the variety of taste sensations and textures it brings. If your guest arrives before preparation is complete, the assembly of delicacies such as bocconcini (miniature balls of Mozzarella) stuffed with sweet sun-dried tomatoes or wrapped in thin slices of herbed eggplant can turn into a joint effort.

Light food is desirable in the early afternoon and tender lamb fillets, cooked with rosemary and white wine, can be ready in about fifteen minutes for a fitting main course. Fresh spinach, braised with butter, pine nuts and nutmeg, takes only five minutes to cook and is a superb but simple complement.

Chocolate and fruit are always popular dessert choices, the stuffed fig dish blends both. Fresh figs are stuffed with dark chocolate, ground almonds and rum, then heated gently for about ten minutes and served in a sea of melted white chocolate. A cheese board laden with Italian cheeses, fresh dates, pears, walnuts and bread is a finale worth sharing.

Left: A selection of Italian cheeses and fresh fruit

ANTIPASTO

Start the meal in style with a colorful platter of antipasto arranged on ginger or grape leaves. Include stuffed artichokes, bocconcini wrapped in herbed eggplant, bocconcini stuffed with sun-dried tomatoes, slices of hot Italian salami and chilled anchovies. Recipes for the artichokes and eggplant follow – the ingredients for the remaining items can be bought from any good Italian delicatessen.

To assemble the platter of antipasto: drain the chilled anchovies on paper towels. Arrange the stuffed artichokes with the eggplant and bocconcini rolls on a platter, adding slices of salami topped with the chilled anchovies, and slices of bocconcini. Serve the sun-dried tomatoes from the glass jar.

Left: A platter of antipasto

123

EGGPLANT

1 eggplant, sliced
salt
olive oil
1 teaspoon chopped fresh tarragon
1 teaspoon chopped fresh basil
4 slices bocconcini, about ½ inch wide

Slice the eggplant, salt lightly and let it stand on paper towels for about 20 minutes. Fry the slices in olive oil for 3 minutes, using enough oil to cover the eggplant slices. Add tarragon and basil and allow to cool.

When the slices are cold, top each with a slice of bocconcini and roll up, securing with cocktail sticks if necessary. Arrange on the antipasto platter.

STUFFED ARTICHOKES

2 artichokes
stuffing:
½ cup fresh white bread crumbs
2 tablespoons toasted pine nuts
2 tablespoons grated Parmesan cheese
to serve:
a little virgin olive oil
freshly grated Parmesan cheese

Trim the artichokes and remove the coarse outside leaves. Place in a steamer over boiling water. Cover and steam for 25 to 30 minutes or until the artichokes are cooked. (The artichokes are cooked when you can easily pull a leaf away.) Allow to cool. Remove the hairy centers or chokes.

To make the stuffing: place the bread crumbs, nuts and Parmesan in a blender or food processor and work to a paste. Remove some of the flesh from the center of the artichokes and spoon half the stuffing into each artichoke.
To serve: dribble a little olive oil over the stuffing and sprinkle with Parmesan cheese.

Above: Lamb fillets with fresh rosemary served with spinach Milanese-style

124

LAMB FILLETS WITH FRESH ROSEMARY

Lamb fillets cooked in this way will be medium rare. Allow more time if you prefer your lamb well done.

2 tablespoons butter
a little oil
1 clove garlic
4 lamb rib eye fillets (the eye of the chops
 from a boned rack of lamb)
4 sprigs fresh rosemary
2 tablespoons white wine
salt
freshly ground pepper
lemon and sprigs of rosemary to garnish

Melt the butter in the oil in a frying pan.

Add the garlic clove, tossing it in the pan for a few minutes to extract the flavour. Discard the garlic. Add the lamb fillets and rosemary and keep turning the meat as you cook for at least 10 minutes or until done to your liking. Transfer the lamb fillets to a heated dish and keep warm.

Add the wine, salt and pepper to the pan and reduce the liquid to a sauce consistency by boiling rapidly. Return the lamb fillets to the pan and quickly toss to coat them in the sauce.

To serve: slice the lamb and serve immediately with spinach and a little sauce. Garnish with rosemary and lemon.

SPINACH MILANESE-STYLE

1½ lb fresh spinach
1 tablespoon butter
¼ cup pine nuts
salt
freshly ground pepper
a pinch of freshly grated nutmeg

Discard the tough stems of the spinach and wash the leaves in water; change the water 2 or 3 times until all the grit is removed. Place them in a large heavy-bottomed saucepan with only the water that clings to the leaves and bring to the boil. Drain the spinach in a colander and run it briefly under cold water. With your hands, squeeze the water out of the spinach.

Melt the butter in a saucepan, add the spinach and mix until well coated with butter. Add the pine nuts. Add salt, pepper and nutmeg to taste. Cook, turning constantly, for about 5 minutes. Transfer to a hot serving dish and serve immediately.

STUFFED FIGS

The figs are very rich so you will probably only require one each – but they are so delicious that we've allowed for two.

4 ripe fresh figs
filling:
3 oz semisweet chocolate
2 tablespoons ground almonds
½ teaspoon rum
3 oz white chocolate
a dash of milk

Cut the tops off the figs and place the figs on a flat ovenproof platter. Grate the dark chocolate into a bowl, add the ground almonds and rum and mix together to a paste. Make a hole down the center of each fig. Press a little of the paste into the center of each fig and spread more paste evenly on top. Place in a preheated 225° oven for about 10 minutes, or until the figs are heated. Do not allow the chocolate to melt.

Melt the white chocolate in the top of a double boiler set over simmering water. Add a little milk. Remove the figs from the oven, pour a little of the white chocolate sauce around each and serve.

Left: Stuffed figs

125

Garden Salad with Scallops and Ginger

Pan-broiled Filets Mignons
Pasta with Zucchini Shreds
Raw Tomato Sauce

Orange Cream

Brie with Dates, Muscatels and Guava Paste

MIDWEEK DINNER
─────FOR FOUR─────

I f time is short, organization is essential. This menu was designed for the busy cook, who perhaps is juggling a job and bringing up a family, but still delights in serving intimate dinners for four on weekday nights – with limited advance preparation.

Careful shopping is the key here. Ingredients like almonds, muscatels and water biscuits are plucked straight from the emergency shelf. Vegetables and the filets mignons can be bought a day ahead, if required, but the scallops, fresh pasta, cheese and pastries should be picked up on the day of the meal.

A healthy salad, featuring as many different greens as possible, is arranged in an attractive, but not too perfect-looking design. A few poached scallops and pieces of shredded ginger add substance and bite.

Individual 2-inch filets mignons, wrapped in bacon, cook quickly and pasta tossed together with shreds of zucchini provides a simple accompaniment. A raw tomato sauce, made Mexican-style with plenty of fresh coriander, adds zest.

The orange cream to follow is fruity, but not too filling. An organized cook can leave the orange rind macerating in the cream and milk overnight in the refrigerator and then bake the custards before work.

A platter of cheeses, dried fruit and nuts served with coffee is elevated to the unusual by the addition of Mexican guava paste which can be made beforehand.

GARDEN SALAD WITH SCALLOPS AND GINGER

¾ lb scallops
½ cup dry vermouth
2½ cups water
1 tiny piece fresh ginger, shredded
5 oz snow peas
5 oz tiny green beans
6 nasturtium leaves
1 small head Bibb lettuce
1 small head Belgian endive, separated into
  leaves
1 small bunch curly endive
1 bulb fennel, thinly sliced in rings
1 ripe avocado
2 Kirby cucumbers, sliced lengthwise
3 oz bean sprouts
6 whole chives
dressing:
⅓ cup white vinegar
¼ cup olive oil
⅓ cup light polyunsaturated oil
1 teaspoon light soy sauce
½ teaspoon sesame oil
1 small clove garlic, crushed
1 small piece fresh ginger, shredded

garnish:
2 or 3 nasturtium flowers
a few leaves of salad burnet (or other herbs)

Place the scallops, vermouth and ½ cup water in a saucepan with half the shredded ginger (reserving the remainder). Bring gently to the boil, reduce the heat and simmer for no more than 1 minute. Drain the scallops and set them aside in a bowl to cool.

In each of 2 small saucepans, bring 1 cup of water to the boil. Add the snow peas to one pan and the beans to the other. After 2 minutes, drain the snow peas and refresh them under cold water to arrest further cooking. Allow the beans to cook for 4 minutes, then drain and refresh them in the same way. Drain both vegetables thoroughly again and set them aside.

To make the dressing: in a screw-top jar, combine all the ingredients, close the lid and shake vigorously until well mixed.

Set aside at room temperature.

Just before serving, assemble the greens on a large platter. In the center, place the largest, flattest nasturtium and lettuce leaves. Add the remaining lettuce and nasturtium leaves with the Belgian endive and curly endive, overlapping the leaves and radiating them outwards. Crisscross with the snow peas, green beans and fennel. Peel and pit the avocado and slice it lengthwise. Arrange it, with the cucumbers, on top of the salad.

Put the poached scallops on top, sprinkle with the bean sprouts and top with the whole chives and reserved shreds of ginger. Garnish the platter with the nasturtium flowers and salad burnet.

Shake the dressing again and drizzle some over the salad, making sure the scallops are glistening. Serve the salad immediately, offering extra dressing in a small glass pitcher.

Left: Garden salad with scallops and ginger

PAN-BROILED FILLET STEAK

4 slices filet mignon, 2 inches thick
4 slices bacon
2 tablespoons butter
4 teaspoons oil

Roll each piece of fillet in a slice of bacon, securing each with a cocktail stick.

In a heavy frying pan, heat the butter and the oil. When it sizzles, add the steaks and sear over high heat for 1 minute on each side. Then reduce the heat slightly and fry to suit individual preferences – allow 2 to 3 minutes on each side for rare steak, 5 to 6 minutes each side for medium steaks and 8 to 10 minutes for well-done steaks. Serve immediately with raw tomato sauce and pasta (recipes follow).

RAW TOMATO SAUCE

You can use a food processor to chop the onion and coriander for this Mexican sauce, but the tomato must be diced by hand.

2 large firm, ripe tomatoes, diced
1 small white onion, chopped finely
about ½ bunch fresh coriander, chopped finely
a pinch of sugar
1 teaspoon oil

Mix all the ingredients together in a small bowl. Serve immediately.
Variation: this sauce is equally delicious cooked. Fry the onion in the oil for 3 minutes, add the tomato and sugar and cook over low heat for 10 minutes more, then stir in the coriander and serve.

PASTA WITH ZUCCHINI SHREDS

½ lb fresh pasta
salt
4 baby zucchini
1 tablespoon butter
2 tablespoons freshly grated Parmesan cheese, to serve

Bring a large pan of salted water to the boil, add the pasta and cook for 3 to 5 minutes until tender but still firm to the bite.

Meanwhile, cut the zucchini in half, scoop out a little of each center and cut the green shells into matchstick strips. Place in a heatproof bowl, cover with boiling water, then immediately drain and refresh under cold water. Drain thoroughly again.

When the pasta is cooked, drain it thoroughly. Melt the butter in the clean pan and return the pasta to it with the zucchini. Heat for 1 or 2 minutes, tossing the pasta constantly. Transfer to a heated serving dish and sprinkle with Parmesan. Serve immediately.

Left: Pan-broiled filet mignon served with raw tomato sauce and pasta with zucchini shreds

ORANGE CREAM

Custard pots are used in this recipe. However, any small ovenproof dishes can be substituted but do check their capacity first. It may be necessary to increase the quantity of ingredients used.

1½ cups cream
1½ cups milk
grated rind of 1½ oranges (some on
*   fine grating section, some on coarser*
*   holes)*
3 egg yolks
2 tablespoons sugar
1 tablespoon Cointreau
to decorate:
4 tiny slices of kumquat
4 sprigs of kumquat leaves

Put the cream and milk into a heavy-bottomed saucepan with the orange rind. Bring to just below the boiling point, then remove from the heat. The rind, if left in the milk, will give it a slightly tart orange flavor – you may wish to strain the milk to remove it at this point.

In a large bowl, beat together the egg yolks, sugar and Cointreau until well mixed, then slowly pour on the scalded milk and cream, stirring constantly.

Arrange 4 small custard cups in a roasting pan and pour cream mixture into each cup, filling to the brim (the custard will subside a little while baking). Pour boiling water into the roasting pan to a depth of ½ inch. Place the pan in a preheated 325° oven and bake for 40 to 50 minutes, reducing the heat to 300° if the tops start to brown too quickly. The creams are ready when the tops are golden brown and a fine skewer inserted in the center of the cream comes out clean.

Remove the creams from the water bath, allow them to cool, then cover and chill in the refrigerator until required. Just before serving, decorate each cream with a tiny slice of kumquat and a sprig of kumquat leaves.

GUAVA PASTE FROM MEXICO

Make this well ahead when guavas are in season. This quantity makes enough for several meals, and will keep for ages. Serve it with Brie, fresh cream cheese or cottage cheese and a basket of muscatels, fresh dates and nuts.

1 lb guavas
¾ cup cold water
2¼ cups (1 lb) sugar

Cut the guavas in half. Scoop out the seeds into a small bowl. Add ½ cup cold water and set the seeds aside to soak.

Put the guavas in a heavy-bottomed saucepan with about ¼ cup water. Bring to the boil, then reduce the heat and simmer for about 20 minutes or until really soft, stirring frequently to prevent scorching.

Strain the water from the seeds (it will be slightly jellylike) and add it to the cooked guavas. Discard the seeds. Put the guavas with the water in which they were cooked, into the container of a blender or food processor. Purée to a pulp. Transfer the guava pulp to a measuring cup, add an equal amount of

sugar and mix well. Transfer to a heavy-bottomed saucepan set over low heat and cook, stirring frequently with a wooden spoon for about 30 minutes until thick – a little dropped on an ice cube should set in a fairly firm lump.

Remove from heat and beat the mixture with a wooden spoon until it forms a heavy paste. Line a square or oblong cake pan with waxed paper and pour the paste into the pan. Set aside in a cool place for 24 hours, protected by cheesecloth (so it can dry out). Ideally it should be dried in the sun for a couple of days after turning out of the pan, or in a preheated 275° oven. Unless the paste is really sticky this probably won't be necessary. Cut it in small squares to serve.

Note: It is vital that you use the correct quantity of sugar, otherwise the guava paste will not set. The paste can be frozen successfully.

Above: Brie with dates, muscatels and guava paste
Left: Orange cream

129

ITALIAN SUPPER
FOR SIX

Baby Radishes
Pasta with Creamy Fresh Herb Sauce
Shrimp Brochettes

Chinese Long Beans with Sweet Red Pepper

Mascarpone with Liqueur

Here is a menu for those of you with bare refrigerators, who suddenly have to cater for unexpected dinner guests. Spur-of-the-moment entertaining is often easier and looks more impressive if you center it around a theme. In many cities fresh pasta shops and traditional Italian delicatessens stay open late making last-minute quests for elusive ingredients simpler.

Start the meal with baby radishes, which are dipped into crocks of butter and salt. Fresh pasta, despite its simplicity, is always popular and an ideal dish to add substance, particularly if the butcher shops are closed. The most basic topping: Parmesan cheese swirled into cream with plenty of fresh herbs for flavor.

Shrimps marinated for twenty minutes in oils and flavorings can be broiled very quickly. Served with Chinese long beans and sweet red peppers for a crisp assembly of green and red.

Mascarpone, the rich Italian cream cheese, requires little doctoring. Form it into "nest" shapes and fill the center with some Amaretto liqueur before serving with fresh figs. The whole meal is deceptively simple and just as scrumptious as one that has been planned for days.

BABY RADISHES

*1 bunch radishes, coarse section of tops
   removed*
½ cup unsalted butter
coarse sea salt

Prepare the radishes and plunge them into icy cold water. Ladle the butter into a crock and pour salt into another crock. Place the crocks on a platter. Arrange the radishes around the crocks and serve so that guests may dip the radishes firstly into the butter then into the salt.

PASTA WITH CREAMY FRESH HERB SAUCE

1 lb fresh green angel's hair or vermicelli
sauce:
1½ cups cream
4 tablespoons clarified butter
½ teaspoon salt
a pinch of grated nutmeg
a pinch of cayenne pepper
*¼ cup freshly grated good quality Parmesan
   cheese*
*1 cup finely chopped mixed fresh herbs (basil,
   thyme, watercress, Italian parsley,
   marjoram and chives)*

To make the sauce: place the cream, butter, salt, nutmeg and cayenne in a heavy-bottomed saucepan and simmer over a low heat for 15 minutes. Whisk in cheese and herbs and simmer while you cook the pasta in plenty of boiling salted water until "al dente", cooked but still firm.

When the pasta is cooked, drain it and divide it among 4 individual bowls. Top with the sauce and serve immediately.

Far left: Pasta with creamy fresh herb sauce

131

CHINESE LONG BEANS WITH SWEET RED PEPPERS

1 lb Chinese long beans, ends trimmed and cut in half
2 tablespoons butter
1 sweet red pepper, seeded and chopped

Place the beans in a steamer over boiling water and cook until just tender, about 5 minutes. Melt the butter in a frying pan over gentle heat, add the beans, toss swiftly to coat and transfer the mixture to a heated serving platter. Serve garnished with chopped sweet red pepper.

MASCARPONE WITH LIQUEUR

This simplest of all finales is irresistible. It can be served with any fruit of your choice. Try peaches or strawberries in place of the figs suggested here.

6 oz Mascarpone cream cheese
powdered sugar to taste
$\frac{1}{3}$–$\frac{1}{2}$ cup Amaretto liqueur
8 fresh figs for serving

In a bowl, mix the cheese and powdered sugar together until blended – the mixture should not be too sweet. Stir in some of the Amaretto. Do not add too much as the cheese must be able to hold the shape of a nest.

Arrange a mound on each of 6 dessert plates. Swirl each into shape and make a hollow in the centers with a spoon. Just before serving, fill the centers of the nests with the remaining liqueur. Serve with fruit.

SHRIMP BROCHETTES, ADRIATIC STYLE

$1\frac{1}{2}$ lb small shrimps
$3\frac{1}{2}$ tablespoons olive oil
$3\frac{1}{2}$ tablespoons vegetable oil
$\frac{2}{3}$ cup fine, dry unflavored bread crumbs
$\frac{1}{2}$ teaspoon very finely chopped garlic
2 teaspoons finely chopped parsley
$\frac{3}{4}$ teaspoon salt
freshly ground pepper, 5 or 6 twists of the mill
lemon wedges

Preheat the broiler to its maximum setting. (The broiler must be heated at least 15 minutes before the shrimps are to be cooked.)

Shell and devein the shrimps. Wash in cold water and pat thoroughly dry with paper towels.

Put the shrimps in a comfortably large mixing bowl. Add as much of the two oils (mixed in equal parts) and of the bread crumbs as you need to obtain an even, light creamy coating on all the shrimps. (Do not add it all at once because it may not be necessary, but if you are working with very tiny shrimps, you may need even more. In that case, always use 1 part olive oil to 1 part vegetable oil.) When the shrimps are well coated, add the chopped garlic, parsley, salt, and pepper and mix well. Allow the shrimps to steep in the marinade for at least 20 minutes at room temperature. Have ready some flat, double-edged skewers. Skewer the shrimps lengthwise, 5 or more shrimps per brochette, depending upon the size. As you skewer each shrimp, curl and bend one end inward so that the skewer goes through the shrimp at three points. This is to make sure that the shrimps won't slip as you turn the skewer.

These shrimps require brisk, rapid cooking. Wait until the grill has been on for 15 minutes. Cook the shrimps no more than 3 minutes on one side and 2 minutes on the other, and even less if the shrimps are very small. Each side is done as soon as a crisp golden crust forms.

Serve piping hot, on the skewers, with lemon wedges on the side.

Above: Shrimp brochettes, Adriatic style;
Chinese long beans with red pepper
Right: Mascarpone with liqueur

132

MEDITERRANEAN BARBECUE

──FOR SIX──

Melanzanesalata

Pita Bread

Risotto con Melone

Souvlakia with Nasturtium Leaves and Yoghurt

Salad of Ruccola

Fresh Fruit and Cheese

I n summer, impromptu entertaining can take place around the grill where the prosaic sausage is gradually being displaced by more exotic grilled meats. This Mediterranean-inspired menu is based on the philosophy of maximizing life's pleasures. A corruption of Greek, Italian and other exotic influences, it is uncomplicated to prepare and can be served in true North Italian manner – in other words, it is a meal that is simple, unhurried but subtly orchestrated so that diners eat lightly, but enjoy it all the more.

Melanzanesalata, a dip made of grilled eggplants, is served with pita bread, radishes and olives to take the edge off appetites as later courses are prepared.

Risotto with canteloupe may seem an unusual combination, but the firm texture and sweet fresh taste of the fruit blends well with the cheese and rice. The canteloupe is stirred in just before serving so that it warms but does not cook. This course can be prepared while the souvlakia marinate, before being cooked quickly on a red hot barbecue. Souvlakia are eaten wrapped in nasturtium leaves – an early but authentically Mediterranean-tasting combination.

A salad of ruccola is enlivened with anchovies and toasted, slivered almonds. Nuts and salad greens work well together. Ruccola leaves are fine, feathery and crisp tasting, rather like arugula or watercress, either of which may be substituted.

Fresh fruit and cheese are the most suitable dessert, followed by steaming cups of freshly made espresso coffee.

Left: Fresh fruit and cheese platter

MELANZANESALATA
(Eggplant dip)

4 medium-sized eggplants
1 clove garlic, crushed
juice of $\frac{1}{2}$ lemon
4 tablespoons olive oil
salt
freshly ground pepper
a handful of chopped parsley
24 Italian black olives, seeded and chopped
garnish:
black olives
6 radishes
pita bread

Prick the eggplants with a skewer and grill over hot coals, turning frequently until the outside skin is charred, or arrange in a roasting pan and bake in a preheated 350° oven for about 1 hour. Remove from the oven and set aside to cool.

Cut the eggplants in half and scoop out the flesh, chop and drain off any liquid.

Place the eggplant flesh in a bowl with the crushed garlic. Mix well with a fork. Add the lemon juice and then the oil, drop by drop. Fold in salt and pepper, parsley and chopped olives carefully.

Serve with black olives, radishes and pita bread to dip.

RISOTTO CON MELONE
(Risotto with Canteloupe)

$\frac{1}{2}$ cup butter
1 small onion, chopped finely
1 lb Arborio rice
salt
freshly ground pepper
1 glass dry white wine
8 cups chicken stock
$\frac{1}{4}$ cup freshly grated Parmesan cheese
a few drops of Tabasco sauce
1 small very ripe canteloupe, peeled, seeded
*   and diced (reserve juice)*

Melt half the butter in a large, heavy flameproof casserole. Add the onion and cook over a moderate heat for 3 to 5 minutes until the onion is soft and golden. Add the rice, salt and pepper and stir with a wooden fork until the fork is completely covered with the mixture. Add the wine and cook until it is absorbed. Add the stock, 1 cup at a time, stirring frequently until the rice absorbs the liquid. Keep the consistency creamy

Above left: Melanzanesalata
Left: Risotto con melone

and, after about 15 minutes, test the rice. It must be "al dente" – tender but still firm to the bite – never soft and mushy.

When the rice is cooked, remove it from the heat and stir in the remaining butter, the cheese and Tabasco sauce. Add the diced canteloupe and juice. Transfer to a heated dish and allow to stand for a minute before serving.

SOUVLAKIA WITH NASTURTIUM LEAVES

Nasturtium leaves, with their peppery flavor, make perfect edible holders for the hot souvlakia. In addition to the leaves garnishing each plate, have a large bowl of leaves and flowers on the barbecue table so that guests can help themselves.

3 lb boned shoulder of veal, diced and trimmed
marinade:
3 tablespoons olive oil
juice of ½ lemon

a few bay leaves
salt
freshly ground pepper
1 teaspoon powdered cumin
1-inch piece fresh ginger, chopped
to serve:
¾ cup yogurt
12 large nasturtium leaves and flowers

To make the marinade: combine all the ingredients in a shallow nonmetallic bowl.

Add the veal cubes, stir and set aside to marinate for a few hours. Drain the meat, reserve the marinade, and thread meat on skewers. Place on a barbecue grill over very hot coals, or under a preheated broiler at maximum heat and cook, turning frequently, basting with the reserved marinade until cooked to your liking.

To serve: place the meat on a platter lined with nasturtium leaves and flowers. Serve with a pot of yogurt. Guests remove the meat from the skewers and wrap each chunk in a nasturtium leaf before dipping it in yogurt to eat.

SALAD OF RUCCOLA

Ruccola has fine feathery leaves and tastes a little like watercress. If you are unable to find any, substitute arugula or watercress.

leaves of ruccola
6 anchovies, torn into shreds
4 tablespoons toasted slivered almonds
dressing:
½ cup good quality olive oil
2 tablespoons tarragon vinegar
1 clove garlic, crushed
2 teaspoons soy sauce
salt
freshly ground pepper

Arrange the ruccola leaves, anchovies and almonds in a serving bowl. Mix the dressing ingredients, toss the salad and serve at once.

Above: Souvlakia with nasturtium leaves

Fish Ball Soup

Decorative Vegetable Salad
Barbecued Duck with Noodles
or
Oriental Chicken

Coconut Ice Cream
Gingered Mangoes and Lychees

ORIENTAL SUPPER
FOR FOUR

Consider oriental food when required to entertain in style at the last minute. Many large cities have late-closing Chinatown areas that are a goldmine for the cook because they stock everything from complete take-out meals to exotic dried, canned and fresh ingredients. This tasty supper has been designed for minimum effort and maximum effect.

Fish ball soup, prepared in almost no time, is followed by crispy barbecued duck with ginger and bamboo shoots or oriental chicken. Fresh coconut ice cream is a palate-cleansing dessert that is followed by Chinese fruits and fortune cookies.

When shopping in Chinatown, arm yourself with a shopping list but do not be too inflexible; leave room to improvise if you see something inspiring. If you are serving the duck rather than the chicken, the shopping list should include one barbecued duck (ask the Chinese butcher to chop it in the traditional Chinese manner), plus soy sauce, hoi sin sauce, Chinese chicken stock, Chinese noodles, fresh coriander, a bunch of green onions, one sweet red pepper, one can of water chestnuts, one can of bamboo shoots, a small head of broccoli, a few snow peas, baby mushrooms, preserved red ginger, one package of prepared uncooked fish balls, coconut ice cream (from a late-closing ice cream parlor), one coconut, one can of lychees, Chinese red salted dates, Chinese black dates, crystallized ginger, ginger in syrup and a box of fortune cookies.

In this menu the shopping is the difficult part; the meal itself requires minimum preparation.

Left: Fish ball soup

FISH BALL SOUP

6 cups water
2 teaspoons instant chicken broth powder
  (Chinese style)
¾ lb fresh white fish balls
garnish:
4 green onions, chopped
1 small piece of fresh ginger, peeled and
  shredded

Pour the water into a large saucepan, whisk in the instant broth and bring to the boil.

Lower the fish balls carefully into the broth and heat gently. Ladle into heated soup bowls and serve garnished with chopped green onions and the shredded fresh ginger.

DECORATIVE VEGETABLE SALAD

1 small head broccoli, cut into flowerets
1 × ¼ lb snow peas
1 sweet red pepper, seeded and sliced finely
8-oz can water chestnuts, drained and sliced
6 oz fresh button mushrooms
dressing:
5 tablespoons walnut oil
1 tablespoon fresh lemon juice
salt
freshly ground pepper
soy sauce to taste

Bring two small saucepans of salted water to the boil. Add the broccoli flowerets to the first pan and cook for 4 to 5 minutes. Drain and immediately plunge into cold water to arrest cooking and set color. Add the snow peas to the second pan, cook for 1 minute, then treat in the same way as the broccoli. Drain both vegetables thoroughly and arrange them, together with the red pepper and water chestnuts in rows on a platter.

Pour the dressing ingredients into a screw-top jar, cover and shake well. Sprinkle the dressing over the vegetables and serve.

Right: Decorative vegetable salad
Below: Barbecued duck with noodles

BARBECUED DUCK WITH NOODLES

1 3-lb freshly barbecued duck, chopped in the Chinese manner
1 piece preserved ginger, sliced finely
¼ cup bamboo shoots, sliced finely
1 lb cooked Chinese noodles
2 tablespoons butter
a few sprigs of fresh coriander
2 green onions, chopped
individual side dishes for serving sauces, such as plum sauce, hoi sin, soy sauce

Arrange the barbecued duck on a serving platter, garnish with sliced ginger and bamboo shoots, cover with foil and re-heat in a preheated 350° oven for 15 to 20 minutes.

Just before serving, bring a pan of water to the boil, add the noodles and reheat them for 3 minutes. Drain the noodles and return them to the pan with the butter, coriander and green onions. Place over gentle heat, and cook until the butter has melted, tossing the mixture constantly.

Transfer to a heated dish and serve immediately with the duck and individual bowls of sauces.

ORIENTAL CHICKEN

This dish can also be prepared using 1 lb flank or fillet steak, cut paper thin, or 12 raw jumbo shrimp.

marinade:
about ¼ cup soy sauce
1 small piece of ginger, crushed
2 cloves garlic, crushed
for the chicken:
3 boned chicken breasts, cut in thin strips
1 teaspoon sesame oil
3 or 4 shallots, chopped

1 sweet red pepper or 2 tomatoes, cut in long
strips
8 green onions
16 snow peas or 16 green beans
1 corn on the cob, kernels stripped and
reserved
4 cups hot cooked long-grain rice to serve

Combine all the marinade ingredients in a shallow non-metallic bowl. Add the chicken strips. The marinade should just cover the meat – if it is too shallow, add more soy sauce. Cover the dish and set aside at room temperature for 1 or 2 hours.

Heat a wok or heavy-bottomed frying pan and add a small amount of sesame oil. Add the shallots and sweet red pepper and the white part of the green onions, cut into fine rings. Stir-fry for 1 minute, then add the chicken with the marinade and cook for about 3 minutes more. Add the snow peas and corn and stir-fry for 2 minutes – all the vegetables are cooked quickly to remain crisp and fresh. Transfer to a heated platter, garnish with the green onions and serve immediately with the rice.

COCONUT ICE CREAM

1 quart coconut ice cream
1 fresh coconut, flesh removed from shell and
grated coarsely

Scoop the ice cream on to serving plates and decorate with the grated coconut. *Note:* If coconut ice cream is unavailable, make your own by combining 1 quart vanilla and 1 cup canned coconut milk. Mix together, pour into a container, cover and freeze. Serve as above.

GINGERED MANGOES AND LYCHEES

2 large ripe mangoes, peeled and cut into bite-
sized pieces
4 canned or fresh lychees, peeled
1 × 1-inch piece of fresh ginger, peeled and
finely slivered
juice and rind of 1 lime
¼ cup honey

Arrange the mangoes and lychees in 4 individual serving bowls and sprinkle with ginger. Pour a little lime juice over the fruit, scatter with lime rind and drizzle with honey. Mix gently and let stand at room temperature for at least 1 hour before serving.

Top right: Coconut ice cream
Right: Chinese fruits and fortune cookies

141

Summer Soup

Pasta with Bacon, Mushroom and Garlic Sauce
Green Salad

Raspberry Fool

STYLISH LUNCH
—FOR EIGHT—

I f friends are to drop by in the morning, it is fun to be able to ask them to stay for lunch, and even more fun to be able to offer something considerably more stylish than sandwiches. However, in such cases, preparation time is limited and so recipes that are quick to prepare are essential. This lunch menu is designed for summer and could be eaten alfresco at an attractively decorated table.

Cans of good-quality beef consommé are an asset to have on the emergency shelf. Add shrimps (easily acquired from the local supermarket), cucumber and mint for a refreshingly light soup that, when chilled and served with brown bread, makes a perfect start to a meal.

Pasta is a no-trouble-at-all main course. The sauce of bacon, mushroom and garlic could be cooked the night before if you have advance warning that you will be catering, although the cream and cheese should be added at the last minute. Made from scratch, the sauce takes about 45 minutes to cook, which is considerably longer than the pasta. The accompaniment: a crisp green salad.

After pasta, a clean-tasting dessert should be scheduled, such as raspberry fool which can be made with fresh or frozen berries. Be careful to taste this dish for sugar as frozen or fresh fruit often requires more sugar than specified. This dessert needs to be made several hours in advance as it has to set. Place it in the coldest part of the refrigerator.

SUMMER SOUP

3 10½-oz cans good condensed consommé
2½ consommé cans of water
1 lb peeled shrimps
1 cucumber, peeled and sliced finely
2 bunches mint, chopped finely
salt
freshly ground pepper

Place the consommé and water in a large tureen or bowl, stir, and gently mix in shrimps, cucumber, mint and salt and pepper to taste. Chill for at least 2 hours before serving with thinly sliced brown bread and butter, cut in quarters.

Left and far left: Summer soup

PASTA WITH BACON, MUSHROOM AND GARLIC SAUCE

2 lb fresh pasta
salt
a little oil for cooking
sauce:
1 cup oil
½ lb bacon, chopped finely
3–4 large onions, chopped finely
4–6 cloves of garlic, chopped finely
1 lb mushrooms, chopped
1¼ cups cream
1½ cups finely grated Parmesan cheese

salt
freshly ground pepper

To make the sauce: heat the oil in a large, heavy-bottomed saucepan and add the bacon, onions and garlic. Cook over low heat for 20 to 30 minutes – the onions and garlic should become soft and lightly coloured but not brown. Add the mushrooms and cook for a further 10 minutes.
To cook the pasta: bring a large pan of salted water to the boil. Add a little oil then gradually add the pasta to the pan so that the water continues boiling. Cook the pasta until just tender.

Just before serving, add the cream, cheese and seasoning to the sauce, stirring constantly to insure the cheese does not stick on the bottom of the pan. Drain the pasta, transfer it to a large platter and cover it with the sauce. Serve immediately with a simple green salad.

Above: Pasta with bacon, mushroom and garlic sauce

RASPBERRY FOOL

3 envelopes gelatin, softened
a little boiling water
1 pint raspberries
6 cups heavy cream
sugar to taste
brandy to taste
to decorate:
2 cups heavy cream, whipped
brandy to taste

sugar to taste

Dissolve the softened gelatin in boiling water, stirring thoroughly. Purée the raspberries and their juice in a blender or food processor. With the motor still running, add the dissolved gelatin in a steady stream.

Lightly whip the cream with the sugar then add the brandy. Take care; if the brandy is added too soon, the cream will not thicken. Carefully fold in the raspberry purée. When thoroughly mixed transfer to a glass serving bowl and refrigerate, overnight if possible.

To decorate: whip the heavy cream with sugar to taste. When thick, add brandy to taste and use to decorate the fool.

Below: Raspberry fool

SUMMER PICNIC
FOR SIX

Artichoke Hearts in Sour Cream

Lobster with Dill Mayonnaise

Apricot Soufflé with Caramel Almonds

Butter Cookies

L ittle advance planning or last-minute effort is required when preparing this simple but elegant dinner. Equally suitable for serving indoors or outdoors picnic-style, the menu is refreshing, imaginative and light – all prerequisites for a summer meal.

Only the heating of the artichokes and the adding of caramelized almonds to the soufflé need to be done directly before the event.

For spur-of-the-moment entertaining, a cook must rely on ingredients that are on the emergency shelf or in the refrigerator or can be purchased easily. The entrée, which uses canned artichoke hearts, sour cream, canned anchovies and Parmesan cheese, is a deliciously tasty dish that fulfills these requirements.

Lobster is always appreciated and needs only a complementary mayonnaise to enhance its succulent, delicate flesh. Rice and a crisp green salad are suitable accompaniments.

The advent of the food processor has reduced the preparation time required to whisk up a creamy fruit soufflé. Individual cold apricot soufflés are served with fragments of crunchy caramelized almonds and butter cookies, the different textures and tastes blending well together.

Left: Artichoke hearts in sour cream

ARTICHOKE HEARTS IN SOUR CREAM

3 14-oz cans artichoke hearts (allow 3 hearts per person)
4 cups sour cream
Tabasco sauce
1 2-oz can flat anchovy fillets, drained
1 cup freshly grated Parmesan cheese
salt
freshly ground pepper

Drain the artichoke hearts and dry well. Place in an ovenproof dish and cover with sour cream. Sprinkle with Tabasco.

Arrange the anchovy fillets over the sour cream in a lattice pattern and sprinkle liberally with Parmesan cheese. Cook in the center of a preheated 375° oven for 40 minutes.

Brown under a preheated broiler just before serving. If serving at a picnic, cool and refrigerate before packing.

Note: This recipe can also be cooked in individual dishes. (*Pictured left.*)

147

LOBSTER WITH DILL MAYONNAISE

3 egg yolks
1 cup olive oil
juice of half a lemon
salt
freshly ground pepper
½ small onion, chopped very finely
6 sprigs of fresh dill, chopped finely
6 lobsters

To make the dill mayonnaise: Using a whisk, beat the egg yolks and slowly add the oil, beating well until the mixture is thick. Whisk in the lemon juice, salt and pepper, onion and dill. Let the mayonnaise stand for at least 4 hours to allow the flavor of the dill to develop.

Cook the lobsters (see Boiled Crayfish page 37) and allow to cool, or buy freshly cooked lobsters. Remove the flesh from the shell and slice. Mix the lobster flesh with the dill mayonnaise and spoon the mixture back into the lobster shells. Serve at once with a green salad.

Left: Lobster with dill mayonnaise

APRICOT SOUFFLÉ WITH CARAMEL ALMONDS

11 oz dried apricots
½ cup water
1 cup almonds
6 tablespoons packed brown sugar
1 tablespoon water
1 cup apricot liqueur
½ cup heavy cream, whipped
2 egg whites, beaten until holding stiff peaks

Soak the apricots in the ½ cup water for 4 to 6 hours.

Place the almonds on a well-buttered baking sheet. Boil the sugar with the 1 tablespoon water, without stirring, until the mixture is caramel brown. Pour this mixture over the almonds and mix. Leave to set. When the toffee is hard, place it between two tea towels and carefully hammer to separate the nuts; try not to squash them.

Drain the water from the apricots, discarding the water. Purée the apricots with the liqueur in a food processor or blender until smooth. Fold in the whipped cream and then carefully fold in the beaten egg whites. Pour into a serving bowl and chill. Immediately before serving, mix half the nuts into the soufflé and sprinkle the remaining nuts over the top.
Note: Individual soufflé dishes can be used in place of one large bowl.

BUTTER COOKIES
(Makes 36 cookies)

½ cup sugar
½ cup butter
1 egg, beaten
½ teaspoon vanilla
½ teaspoon finely grated lemon rind
1 teaspoon finely grated orange rind
¾ cup flour

Beat the butter and sugar to a cream. Add the egg, vanilla and lemon and orange rind and beat until white and fluffy. Add the flour and mix well.

Drop the small teaspoons of the mixture on to the buttered baking sheets. The cookies will spread during cooking so keep them well apart.

Bake on the center shelf of a preheated 375° oven for 10 minutes or until the cookies are golden brown round the edge.

Below: Apricot soufflé with caramel almonds

149

ENTERTAINING IN STYLE

Call it a banquet, a birthday, a feast or simply a party, celebrating a special occasion provides you with a chance to do two things: put your best food forward and demonstrate that the guest of honor is worth the best that you can give.

Celebrations are to everyday life what froth is to cappuccino. They are the flame in the flambé, the delicate heart of the artichoke. They're not only the frosting on your cake, but the whipped cream, as well.

A special occasion is an indulgent reward for everyone, a time when diets and moderation evaporate like water from the spout of a boiling kettle. And because such an event doesn't come along every day, a little indulgence of this sort will do no harm. A big occasion is a reassurance that fantasy, frivolity and fun are well and truly with us.

One thing is certain. You cannot tackle a big party single-handed. Apart from spirit, innovation and enthusiasm, you will also need a team of aides at your side. Even so, be prepared for first-night jitters.

151

Stuffed Artichokes with Anchovy Sauce

Salad of Julienne Vegetables

Breasts of Quail on Wild Rice

Grand Marnier Sabayon
Tuiles with Chocolate and Violets

CELEBRATION LUNCH
—FOR FOUR—

Τhis delicate culinary collection is a subtle celebration in itself. The meal is a carefully constructed progression through beautifully presented yet strikingly different dishes, all based on good, simple ingredients with fresh, distinctive flavors. None of the courses is heavy. The presentation appears complex, but really only requires care and the investment of a little time.

Exotically flavored artichokes are stuffed with parsley, pine nuts and anchovies and then served with a delicate, moistening, anchovy-flavored cream sauce. The creamy sauce is randomly decorated with tiny chanterelle mushrooms, pink peppercorns, a smidgin of saffron and a fan of red pepper.

Just as attractively presented is the salad of whole and julienne vegetables, which is served before the breasts of quail. These are arranged artistically on a tiny bed of wild rice and surround a basket of julienne potatoes holding a quail egg. Each plate, is garnished with heart-shaped pieces of beet, a few sprigs of herbs and a rich sauce with a deep maroon color.

The dessert is a warm Grand Marnier sabayon, presented in parfait glasses. It should be served immediately, with a web of fine spun sugar topping each. Crisp tuiles, small cookies decorated with chocolate and crystallized violets, are handed around to complement the sabayon's creamy consistency.

Left: Grand Marnier sabayon (page 155)
Above: Stuffed artichokes with anchovy sauce

STUFFED ARTICHOKES WITH ANCHOVY SAUCE

4 tablespoons lemon juice
4 artichokes, trimmed
stuffing:
4 tablespoons chopped parsley
4 teaspoons chopped pine nuts
4 anchovy fillets, chopped
salt
freshly ground pepper
anchovy sauce:
1 cup sour cream
1 cup chicken stock
1 teaspoon Worcestershire or anchovy sauce
garnish:
8 dried chanterelles, soaked in warm water
1 teaspoon pink peppercorns (see Note)
a few shreds of saffron
1 sweet red pepper, cut spirally into long thin strips

To cook the artichokes: bring a large saucepan of water to the boil, add the lemon juice and the artichokes and cook over moderate to high heat for 25 to 35 minutes until tender. The artichokes are ready when you can easily pull a leaf away. Remove from the water, trim off tough outer leaves and part of the stalk. Cut in half lengthwise, paring the stalk to a tapered shape. Remove the choke if necessary.

To make the stuffing: in a bowl, combine all the ingredients and divide stuffing among the artichoke halves placing it in the center of each half. Place 2 stuffed halves on each of 4 individual plates.

To make the sauce: combine all the ingredients in a small heavy-bottomed pan and cook over moderately high heat until reduced and thickened, adding salt and pepper to taste.

To serve: place a small portion of sauce alongside the stuffed artichoke halves on each plate. Garnish by sprinkling the sauce with 2 chanterelles, a few pink peppercorns, a little saffron and a red pepper fan.

Note: Pink peppercorns provoke an allergic reaction in some people.

153

SALAD OF JULIENNE VEGETABLES

This salad can be made from any variety of vegetables. Line a serving bowl with green salad leaves – Belgian endive, blanched snow peas or watercress. Then make julienne strips from green and red sweet peppers, green onions and carrots. To create a curly effect, place them in a bowl of iced water for about 1 hour. Dry well before scattering over the salad leaves.

To finish the salad, sprinkle over a few tiny beet hearts cut from thinly sliced cooked beet. Toss the salad just before serving in a little well-seasoned vinaigrette dressing.

BREASTS OF QUAIL ON WILD RICE

⅔ cup wild rice
oil for deep frying
1–2 potatoes
6 tablespoons butter
12 quail breasts, skinned
sauce:
3 teaspoons red wine vinegar
1 cup red wine
1 cup stock (made from quail bones)
garnish:
4 hard-boiled quail eggs, peeled
cooked beet slices
chopped chives
sprigs of thyme
sage flowers

To prepare the wild rice: follow the package instructions, or use the following method. Wash the rice under cold, running water. Place 3 cups of water in a saucepan and bring to the boil. Add the rice and boil steadily for 5 minutes. Remove from heat, cover the pan and let stand for 1 hour. Drain, rinse and cook in a large pan of boiling salted water until tender – about 35 to 40 minutes.

To make the potato baskets: heat oil for frying in a large saucepan. Cut the peeled potatoes in julienne (matchstick) strips and dry well. Using 2 small strainers, arrange potato strips in a criss-cross fashion in one strainer and gently press the other into it to make a basket shape. Still holding the strainers together, immerse them in the hot oil until golden. Drain on paper towels. Repeat with remaining potato strips to make 3 more baskets.

To cook the quail: melt the butter in a large frying pan, add the quail breasts and cook over low to moderate heat for about 2 minutes on each side or until cooked.

To make the sauce: place the vinegar and

wine in a heavy-bottomed pan and simmer until thickened and reduced by half. Add stock and reduce again. Keep warm.

To serve: place a quarter of the wild rice in the center of each plate. Over this, fan 3 quail breasts, making room in the center for a potato basket. Place a quail egg in each basket and decorate with a piece of beet cut with a heart-shaped cutter. At the last moment, spoon the sauce over the breasts and add a few chopped chives, a sprig of thyme and a sage flower for garnish.

GRAND MARNIER SABAYON

6 egg yolks and 1 whole egg, beaten
⅔ cup sugar (or to taste)
1 tablespoon Grand Marnier
spun sugar:
1 cup sugar
½ cup water

Place the egg yolks with the whole egg in a heatproof bowl over gently boiling water and gradually add the sugar. Beat with a wire whisk or rotary beater until the sauce thickens and reaches a creamy consistency. Stir in the Grand Marnier. Remove from heat but keep the sabayon warm over hot but not simmering water.

To make the spun sugar: place the sugar with the water in a saucepan. Stir over low heat until all the sugar has dissolved, then boil until pale golden. Do not stir once mixture boils. Remove from stove, allow bubbles to subside and prepare to spin.

Meanwhile, spoon sabayon into 4 glasses as the sugar must be spun on the top.

Using the tines of two forks, spin the sugar over the sabayon building a fine pyramid shape. If the sugar becomes brittle, simply reheat gently. Add real violets or candied violets for decoration. Serve with tuiles decorated with chocolate and tiny violets.

TUILES WITH CHOCOLATE AND VIOLETS
(Makes 25–30 biscuits)

½ cup sugar
⅓ cup all-purpose flour
1 teaspoon vanilla
1 egg white
to decorate:
5½ oz semisweet chocolate
fresh violets, pansies or small crystallized flowers

Place all the ingredients for the cookies in a blender or food processor and blend well. (Or place all the ingredients in a large bowl and beat very thoroughly with electric beater.) If the mixture is too thick, add a little more egg white, but not a whole egg white.

Lightly butter a baking sheet and spread teaspoons of the mixture on the sheet, making thin, round shapes some distance apart. Bake in a preheated 400° oven. The cookies should take only about 5 minutes to bake. (They will color around the edges when cooked.) Quickly remove from the sheet with a wooden spatula and form them into a "tuile" shape by rolling the cookies around the greased round handle of a wooden spoon. Place the shaped cookies on a wire rack to cool.

To decorate: melt the chocolate in the top of a double boiler set over simmering water. Remove from water and allow chocolate to cool a little. One at a time, carefully slide the handle of a small teaspoon through each cookie and dip each side in chocolate. Decorate with the fresh violets, pansies or small crystallized flowers.

Top left: Salad of julienne vegetables
Left: Breasts of quail on wild rice
Right: Tuiles with chocolate and violets

155

Rillettes of Chicken
Whole Wheat Bread

Leek Pavé with Ginger Vinaigrette

Rabbit in Mustard and Tarragon
Boiled Baby Potatoes
Steamed Spinach
Spring Salad

Blueberry Soufflés
Nutmeg Ice Cream

Amaretto Chocolate Truffles
Coffee

Dinner For A Summer Evening

FOR EIGHT

The menu for a dinner party should be balanced, colorful and orchestrated for ascending and descending palate surprises. These dishes, designed for a relaxed spring or summer meal, fulfill these requirements and make the most of fresh seasonal ingredients. Conveniently, most of the cooking can be done before the guests arrive, thus allowing the cook to socialize. Rillettes of chicken make a delicious and attractive appetizer, especially if served with a bowl of sour cherries and toasted whole wheat bread cut into heart shapes.

Leek pavé is a striking dish. Baby leeks moistened with a contrasting, tangy ginger vinaigrette are placed in crisscrossed layers of green and white forming a chequered pattern.

Rabbit is a tasty meat that is often overlooked. White rabbit in mustard and tarragon can be prepared up to two days in advance, but be careful not to overcook it or the meat will become stringy. The salad of seasonal vegetables can be served either with the rabbit or after it as a palate-cleansing course. Dribble the vinaigrette over just before serving, but do not toss the salad.

Blueberry soufflés can be prepared in advance and then frozen. Thaw them one hour before serving and then cook until golden. Spicy nutmeg ice cream is served as a fitting contrast.

Left: Rillettes of chicken served with toasted whole wheat bread and sour cherries

---

RILLETTES OF CHICKEN

1 lb cleaned chicken gizzards and hearts (if not available, use ½ lb coarsely minced chicken)
1 sprig fresh thyme
1 bay leaf
freshly ground pepper
1 clove garlic, chopped finely
½ cup unsalted butter
1 cup cold water
sea salt
to serve:
whole wheat bread, crusts removed and cut into heart shapes
sour cherries

Put the gizzards and hearts in a food processor or blender with the thyme leaves and process until coarsely chopped. Place the mixture in a large heavy frying pan with the remaining ingredients. Simmer, uncovered, over medium low heat, stirring occasionally, for approximately 45 minutes, or until the liquid evaporates.

Drain the mixture through a sieve over a small bowl to catch the fat. Transfer the drained rillettes to another bowl. Cover both mixtures with plastic wrap and refrigerate until the fat is set. (This can be done the day before serving.)

Return the rillettes to the food processor or blender and chop until medium fine, adding the set fat 1 tablespoon at a time. Do not add additional fat until the previous spoonful of fat has been well incorporated. Repeat until all the fat has been added. Adjust the seasoning if necessary. Scrape the mixture into a 1½-cup crock, cover and refrigerate.

Serve with toasted whole wheat bread and sour cherries.
Note: This dish should be made a day in advance to allow for setting and chilling.

157

LEEK PAVÉ WITH GINGER VINAIGRETTE

15 baby leeks, well washed to remove all grit
  and dirt
sea salt
freshly ground pepper
ginger vinaigrette:
2 tablespoons julienne (matchstick) strips of
  preserved ginger
⅓ cup peanut oil
1½ tablespoons red wine vinegar
2 tablespoons soy sauce

Line a rectangular 8½ × 4½ × 2½ inch loaf
pan with a double layer of foil.

Trim the leeks to fit the length of the
prepared pan. Bring a large pan of salted
water to rapid boiling point, add the
leeks and cook until only just tender.
Immediately refresh them under running cold water and drain well. (If the
leeks are overcooked, they will become
stringy and spoil the pavé.)

Arrange a layer of leeks on the bottom
of the pan with all the white parts of the
leeks at one end. Season, then arrange a
second layer, this time with the white
parts of the leeks at the other end; season.
Repeat the layers and seasoning until the
pan is full. Cover with foil and place a
board on top of the foil that fits exactly in
the top of the pan.

With the board in place, invert the
pan on to a large dish and weight it down
with several heavy objects. This will
squeeze out the excess juices. Cover with
foil and refrigerate overnight.

To make the vinaigrette: whisk all the
ingredients together.

To serve: unmold the pavé carefully on to
a larger board and remove the foil. Using
an electric knife, trim the ends of the leeks
to neaten. Cut into 8 even slices and serve
on large flat plates. Spoon a little vinaigrette over one end of each slice and serve
at once.

RABBIT IN MUSTARD AND TARRAGON

¼ cup butter
1 large rabbit, about 4½–5 lb, cut into
  serving pieces, plus the liver (hutch-
  raised rabbits are available at
  specialty game shops)
6½ oz lean smoking ham, cut into 1 inch
  pieces
8 green onions, trimmed and 2-inch green
  tops left attached
1 tablespoon flour
1 cup wholegrain prepared mustard
2 cups dry white wine
sea salt
freshly ground pepper
2 sprigs fresh tarragon

Heat the butter in a large heavy pan
until golden. Add the rabbit pieces a few
at a time and fry until lightly browned on
all sides. Transfer the rabbit to a heavy
casserole. Fry the ham and green onions
in the butter to seal on all sides. Using a
slotted spoon, transfer the ham and
onions to the casserole.

Sprinkle the flour over the rabbit and
mix well with a wooden spatula until all
the pieces are coated. Spoon the mustard
over the top.

Fry the liver for 1 minute on each side
and add to the other ingredients in the
casserole.

Pour the butter out of the pan and
discard. Return the pan to the heat and
deglaze with the wine, scraping up all the
caramelized juices on the bottom of the
pan. Pour into the casserole, season to
taste and put the tarragon sprigs on top.
Cover tightly and cook on the center
shelf of a preheated 400° oven for 45
minutes or until the rabbit is just tender.
Leave to cool, then refrigerate until
required.

On the day the rabbit is to be served,
remove from the refrigerator and bring
to room temperature. Reheat in a preheated 375° oven for 30 minutes or until
hot. Do not overcook or the rabbit will
fall to pieces.

Remove the tarragon and serve the
rabbit with boiled red-skinned potatoes,
steamed and buttered spinach and a
spring salad.

Note: The rabbit can be prepared up to 2
days in advance.

SPRING SALAD

1 small loose-leaf lettuce, well washed,
  crisped in the refrigerator and dried
1 small Belgian endive, washed and dried
1½ cups arugula leaves, freshly picked,
  washed and dried
1 cup watercress sprigs, washed and dried
8 baby nasturtium leaves
½ cup chervil sprigs, washed and dried
1 sweet red pepper
½ sweet yellow pepper
8 baby yellow tomatoes
8 freshly picked violets, preferably picked in
  the sun, so they taste of musk
hazelnut vinaigrette:
¼ cup hazelnut oil
1 teaspoon white wine vinegar

sea salt
freshly ground pepper

Arrange all the salad ingredients and the
chervil in a large glass salad bowl. Broil
the sweet peppers on a baking sheet lined
with foil until blistered all over. Put into
a plastic bag and seal. Set aside for 10
minutes to steam. Peel, remove the seeds
and cut into fine julienne (matchstick)
strips. Arrange over the salad. Dress the
salad with the tomatoes and violets.

To make the vinaigrette: whisk all the ingredients together and drizzle over the
salad at the moment of serving. Do not
toss.

Top: Leek pavé with ginger vinaigrette
Above: Spring salad

BLUEBERRY SOUFFLÉS

scant ½ cup all-purpose flour
1¾ cups milk
1 egg
⅔ cup caster sugar
⅔ cup blueberries, reduced over heat to ⅓ cup
6 large eggs, separated
2 tablespoons melted butter
pinch salt
36 silver dragées
extra butter and sugar for dishes

Use the extra butter and sugar to grease and line 12 one-cup soufflé dishes. Place them on a baking sheet.

Whisk the flour, ¾ cup of the milk and the egg together in a heavy-bottomed pan and cook over low heat until thickened. Stir in the remaining milk, sugar and reduced berry mixture. Beat in the egg yolks, one at a time. Stir in the melted butter.

Beat the egg whites with a few grains of salt until they form firm and glossy peaks. Using a rubber spatula, fold a quarter of the whites into the blueberry mixture. Fold in the remaining whites and spoon into the prepared dishes. Run your finger tip around the top of the soufflés to insure the mixture rises evenly. Scatter with the silver dragées. Freeze if the soufflés are not to be cooked within 30 minutes.

Cook the soufflés on the center shelf of a preheated 400° oven for 12 to 15 minutes or until well risen and golden on top. Serve at once with nutmeg ice cream (recipe follows).
Note: Soufflés can be prepared up to the ready-to-cook stage and stored frozen for up to 3 weeks. Defrost for 1 hour before cooking.

This quantity of mixture is sufficient for 12 small soufflés. Freeze the extra soufflés.

NUTMEG ICE CREAM

4 egg yolks
⅔ cup caster sugar
1 cup milk
2 teaspoons freshly grated nutmeg
1¼ cups heavy cream

Whisk the egg yolks and sugar together in a bowl until the mixture forms "ribbons" (when the whisk is lifted from the mixture it will leave a trail on the surface). Place the milk in a saucepan over medium heat and bring to a simmer; slowly whisk the milk on to the egg yolk mixture. Return the custard to the pan and cook over medium heat, whisking constantly until the mixture thickens. Remove from the heat and cool over iced water. Whisk in the nutmeg. Transfer to a bowl and chill the mixture in the refrigerator.

When the custard is cold, fold the heavy cream in and freeze in an ice cream maker. Spoon into a container, and store, covered, in the freezer for 1 hour before serving.
To serve: 2 minutes before the soufflés are cooked, wet a dessert spoon and roll the ice cream in the spoon by dragging it towards you across the top of the ice cream. Hold the bowl of the spoon in your hand for a few seconds to release the ice cream from the spoon (your blood heat does the trick). Arrange on a large glass plate and place the hot soufflés on the plates beside the ice cream.
Note: If you do not have an ice cream

maker, whip the cream before adding to the custard mixture. Freeze the mixture in ice trays and beat well when the ice cream begins to set.

This ice cream can be made 3 days before serving, provided it is stored covered.

AMARETTO CHOCOLATE TRUFFLES

1 tablespoon milk
2 tablespoons cream
4½ squares semisweet chocolate, grated
1 tablespoon Amaretto liqueur
1½ cups unsweetened cocoa powder

Place the milk and cream in a small heavy-bottomed pan and bring slowly to the boil. Simmer until reduced by half. Add the chocolate and stir over low heat until it melts. Do not allow to boil.

Remove from the heat and stir in the Amaretto. Transfer to a bowl and cool over iced water, stirring from time to time until the mixture reaches the consistency of thick chocolate icing.

With dry hands, shape the mixture into eight large truffles; roll in the cocoa powder, to finish. Leave in a cool place for 1 hour, or store, covered, in the refrigerator.
Note: These can be made 3 days in advance. Bring to room temperature for at least 1 hour before serving with coffee.

Below: Amaretto chocolate truffles
Below left: Blueberry soufflé with nutmeg ice cream

159

MIDWINTER DINNER
—FOR SIX—

Brown Butter Salad

Smoked Salmon and Shrimp Rolls
Buttered Brown Bread

Roast Goose with Wild Rice Stuffing
Fried Chipolata Sausages and Baked Apples
Mixed Vegetables

Festival Fruits
Snowball

For special occasions in winter, substantial fare is warranted. This dinner features a filling main course and dessert, supplemented by several lighter courses. Much of the preparation can be done the day before. A light salad of lettuce, tomato and avocado topped with browned butter (how sinful!) and sesame seeds sets the tone of the meal. Once the butter is added, the salad must be served immediately while it is crisp.

Smoked salmon and shrimp rolls follow. In this case, the tomato sauce, mayonnaise and shrimps can be prepared ahead, but once the rolls are assembled, they must be served within the hour as the mayonnaise and sauce may run together. Crisp, curly endive and bread are served for contrast.

Although goose seems to have fallen from favor, it is a meat well worth trying. A tasty well-textured stuffing of wild rice, apple, celery, prunes and onions fills the large body cavity. No extra fat is needed for roasting as the goose supplies its own as it cooks. Baked apples, chipolata sausages and fresh seasonal vegetables can be served with it.

Two desserts are offered: a refreshing medley of fruit soaked in brandy and honey (made no more than two hours ahead) and a startling improvement on the English plum pudding. The stunning Snowball is, basically, slices of plum pudding topped with vanilla ice cream and hard sauce and then frozen. The dish can be made a few days ahead as it stores well and the alcohol in the sauce prevents it from freezing too hard.

Left: Brown butter salad (page 162)

BROWN BUTTER SALAD

This salad must be served as soon as it is made or the avocado will discolor.

1 head firm-leaved lettuce, outer leaves removed and discarded
3 red tomatoes
1 large firm avocado
8 shallots, sliced finely
salt
freshly ground pepper
½ cup butter
1 tablespoon sesame seeds

Wash the lettuce, dry well then break up lettuce leaves and divide among 6 large plates. Slice each tomato in 4 and place 2 slices on each plate. Peel and slice avocado into 12. Arrange 2 slices on each salad. Sprinkle with shallots and salt and pepper. Melt the butter in a small saucepan. Add the sesame seeds and continue to heat gently until both butter and sesame seeds turn brown. Spoon a little brown butter over each salad and serve immediately.

Above: Smoked salmon and shrimp rolls

SMOKED SALMON AND SHRIMP ROLLS

fresh tomato sauce:
1 tablespoon olive oil
1 onion, peeled and chopped finely
2 tomatoes, peeled, seeded and chopped
3 or 4 leaves fresh basil, chopped
salt
freshly ground pepper
pinch sugar (optional)
mayonnaise:
2 egg yolks
2 teaspoons lemon juice
½ teaspoon hot English mustard
salt
freshly ground pepper
½ cup peanut oil
¾ cup olive oil
salmon rolls:
12 slices smoked salmon
36 cooked shrimps, peeled, cleaned and cut in pieces

¾ cup chopped celery
1 cup mayonnaise
2 tablespoons fresh tomato sauce, or to taste
salt
freshly ground pepper
Tabasco sauce (optional)
garnish:
curly endive

To make the tomato sauce: heat the oil in a frying pan and fry the onion slowly until softened a little. Add the tomatoes, basil, salt and pepper. Cook slowly until the sauce is well reduced and thick. Taste the sauce and add sugar if necessary. Allow to cool thoroughly.
To make the mayonnaise: put the egg yolks, lemon juice, mustard, salt and pepper in the bowl of a food processor or blender and mix well. Gradually add the oils and

mix until the mayonnaise is thick.
To make the salmon rolls: spread slices of smoked salmon on a large board. Mix the shrimps, celery, mayonnaise and fresh tomato sauce. Taste for salt and pepper. Add 1 or 2 drops Tabasco sauce or more tomato sauce for a more tangy filling. Spoon equal amounts of filling on each piece of smoked salmon and roll up. Serve at once, or cover and stand in the refrigerator for not more than 1 hour as the mayonnaise and tomato sauce may run together.

Arrange 2 rolls on each plate and garnish with a few leaves of curly endive. Serve with tiny brown bread-and-butter sandwiches or slices of buttered French bread.

ROAST GOOSE WITH WILD RICE STUFFING

1 dressed goose (about 7½ lb)
2 cups chicken stock
1 cup water
stuffing:
1¼ cups wild rice
3½ cups hot tap water
½ cup plus 1 tablespoon butter
1 teaspoon salt
2 large onions, chopped
2 Delicious or Granny Smith apples, peeled and chopped in chunks
1 cup chopped celery

1½ cups pitted prunes
salt
freshly ground pepper
garnish:
6 very small Granny Smith apples, cored
6 teaspoons butter
½ cup sugar
1 cup white wine
1 tablespoon vegetable oil
18 chipolata sausages

Remove the neck and wing tips from the goose and cut away unnecessary skin from neck end, leaving enough to fold over stuffing in front opening. Dry goose inside and out with paper towels. Cover and stand until goose is at room temperature. Put neck, skin, wing tips, chicken stock and water in a saucepan, bring to the boil, lower the heat, cover and simmer until the meat falls off the bones. Strain the stock into a bowl, discarding the solids in the strainer. Cover the bowl and place it in the refrigerator.
To make the stuffing: put the wild rice, water, 1 tablespoon butter and salt in a

162

saucepan and bring to the boil. Lower the heat, cover and simmer for 30 minutes. If there is any liquid in the pan, strain wild rice and discard liquid. Set the wild rice aside to cool. Melt remaining butter in a frying pan, add the onions and sauté over low heat for 3 to 5 minutes until just softened. Add apple and celery and toss in the butter for a few seconds. Add to the wild rice and stir in the prunes. Mix together lightly and season well with salt and pepper. Stuff front part of goose, fold over skin and secure with poultry pins. Stuff the body cavity with remaining stuffing and sew up opening using double thread and a darning needle.

Place the goose on a rack in a large roasting pan. Sprinkle the skin with salt, rubbing it in well. Do not add any fat.

Bake on the shelf second from the bottom of a preheated 425° oven for 30 minutes. Cover the top of the goose with foil. Lower the heat to 350° and cook for a further 2½ to 3 hours or until a leg pulls' away easily when tested. Baste occasionally during cooking.

Bake the apples for the garnish: about 25 minutes before the goose is ready, place the apples side by side in an ovenproof dish. Add 1 teaspoon butter to each core cavity and sprinkle each apple with a little sugar. Pour in the wine and bake the apples below the goose.

When the goose is cooked, transfer it to a heated platter, cover it lightly with foil and let it stand for 20 minutes before carving, during which time the apples will finish cooking.

To make the sauce: remove the stock from the refrigerator, discard any fat on the surface and measure out 2 cups. Discard the fat in the roasting pan and place the pan over moderate heat. Add the measured stock, and bring to the boil, stirring vigorously to incorporate pan scrapings. Reduce the heat and simmer the sauce until reduced to about 1 cup.

To cook the chipolatas: heat the vegetable oil in a frying pan, add the chipolatas and fry, turning occasionally, for 5 to 8 minutes.

Carve the goose and serve with pan juices, stuffing, chipolatas, a baked apple and vegetables of your choice.

Below: Roast goose with wild rice stuffing, fried chipolata sausages and baked apples

163

PLUM PUDDING

1 cup butter
1 cup sugar
4 eggs
scant ½ cup all-purpose flour
¼ teaspoon ground cinnamon
¼ teaspoon ground cloves
½ teaspoon ground nutmeg
½ teaspoon salt
2 cups fresh white bread crumbs, made from
  3-day-old bread
2 cups raisins
2 cups sultanas
2 cups currants
1 cup crystallized cherries, halved
2 cups mixed peel
1 cup preserved figs
1 cup preserved ginger
1 carrot, grated
grated rind of 2 oranges
grated rind of 1 lemon
1 cup whole blanched almonds
4 tablespoons beer
4 tablespoons brandy

In a large mixing bowl, cream the butter with the sugar. Add the eggs one at a time, beating well after each addition. Add the flour, spices, salt and bread crumbs, and mix well. Finally stir in the remaining ingredients, adding the beer and brandy last.

Place a small circle of buttered parchment paper in the bottom of a large heatproof bowl. Pour in the pudding mixture. Cover the bowl with 2 sheets of heavy foil, pleated down the center and secured with string so that no water can get into the pudding as it cooks.

Place a small circle of buttered parchment paper in the bottom of a large heatproof bowl. Pour in the pudding mixture. Cover the bowl with 2 sheets of heavy foil, pleated down the center and secured with string so that no water can get into the pudding as it cooks.

Store it, covered with fresh foil, in a cool place.

Note: If serving traditionally, reheat the pudding for 2 hours in exactly the same way as before. Turn out on a large plate and serve with hard sauce.

FESTIVAL FRUITS

1 medium honeydew melon
16 or 20 fresh dates, halved and pitted
10 to 12 dessert figs, cut in chunks, stems
  discarded
36 black grapes
36 green grapes
¾ cup brandy
2 tablespoons honey

Cut the melon in half and scrape out the seeds. Cut flesh in small balls with a melon baller. Place the balls in a large glass bowl with the remaining fruits. In a bowl, mix the brandy and honey well and pour over the fruit. Stir through gently. Cover and refrigerate for no more than 2 hours or fruit will lose freshness and the brandy will discolor the melon.

SNOWBALL

This recipe is designed to use up the last of the plum pudding.

sliced pieces of plum pudding
1 quart good-quality vanilla ice cream
hard sauce:
1½ cups powdered sugar
¾ cup unsalted butter
a pinch of salt
¼ cup brandy

Butter an upturned baking sheet and on it draw a circle, 6½ inches in diameter. Cover the circle with slices of pudding, patting them firmly together to make a firm base. Cover with vanilla ice cream and shape pudding like an upturned bowl. Place in the freezer overnight.

To make the hard sauce: place all the ingredients in a bowl and beat until fluffy and light in color. Remove the dessert from the freezer and spread the hard sauce over it to completely cover the ice cream. Return to the freezer and freeze until the hard sauce is firm. Cover with foil and store in the freezer until required. Transfer to a platter and slice it like a cake.

Left: Festival fruits
Right: Snowball

Platter of Canapés

Tomato Timbales with Avocado Purée and Lime Mayonnaise

Squid stuffed with Scallop Mousseline

Roast Squab stuffed with Savory Mousse
Tartelets of Onions and Raisins
Wild Rice
Snow Peas

Chocolate Pecan Torte
Crème Chantilly

ANNIVERSARY DINNER
FOR EIGHT

Advance planning makes it possible to waltz through the preparation of this anniversary dinner. Aside from the shopping, much of the work can be, indeed, needs to be done the day before. For example, the miniature pastries served with drinks, the squid stuffed with scallop mousseline and the squab all need to be refrigerated overnight. Although the squid recipe requires care, it is not as complex to make as it may seem.

This is a well-coordinated menu that should be served in its entirety for maximum effect as all the courses complement one another. The diners start with a selection of canapés, which are served with rosé Champagne and include tiny pieces of smoked eel rolled with cream cheese laced with Japanese green horseradish (wasabi), quail eggs and deep-fried slices of herb bread.

The next course of tomato timbales served with avocado purée and lime mayonnaise is smooth and rich – a few delicate mouthfuls. These are followed by stuffed squid and then the more substantial roast squab, stuffed with duck liver and apple mousse and served with nutty-tasting wild rice, steamed snow peas and tartelets filled with a confit of shallots and raisins. The mousse and stock should be made the day before and the squabs marinated overnight in a potent mix of seasoned maple syrup, soy sauce and red wine. The squabs take little time to cook before serving.

Chocolate pecan torte, a grand finale, has a dense, moist, but interesting texture as the pecans are hand chopped so that they remain uneven. Serve the cake with homemade ice cream (preferably coffee or Grand Marnier) or crème Chantilly.

PLATTER OF CANAPÉS

Serve a selection of the following on a large platter . . .

Smoked eel triangles: skin and fillet smoked eel. If the eel is particularly thick, slice it in half lengthwise and cut it again into 5-inch lengths. Spread each fillet with a thin layer of cream cheese which has been creamed with Japanese green powdered horseradish (wasabi) to taste. Roll up and slice through. Serve on triangles of rye bread, each garnished with a caper.

Quail and bean sprout pyramids: bring quail eggs to the boil, then cool in running cold water. Shell and place in sterilized jars. Pour in your favorite, slightly sweet spiced vinegar mixture. Seal and store in the refrigerator. To serve, pile bean sprouts on to bread croutons and place the halved hard-boiled quail eggs on top. To make the croutons, cut discs from ½-inch thick slices of herb bread with a cookie cutter. Fry in butter until crisp, drain on paper towels.

Sesame cheese pastries: reroll leftover pieces of puff pastry and cut into small discs with a cookie cutter. Cream Roquefort cheese with a little Cognac and cream cheese, or mash anchovies preserved in oil with cream cheese. Spoon a little filling on to the pastry discs. Fold in half into miniature pasties, seal, glaze with beaten egg and sprinkle with sesame seeds. Place on a baking sheet and cook in a preheated 425° oven for 20 minutes or until golden. (*Pictured left.*)

TOMATO TIMBALES WITH AVOCADO PURÉE
AND LIME MAYONNAISE

¼ cup olive oil
8 large red tomatoes, chopped roughly
4 shallots, chopped
½ cup Madeira
1 teaspoon sugar
freshly ground pepper
a few sprigs of basil, chopped
8 eggs
1 cup cream
1 to 2 avocados
lime juice to taste
extra cream
1 cup mayonnaise made with fresh lime juice
* and lime mustard instead of vinegar or*
* lemon juice*

Heat the oil in a saucepan over gentle heat and cook the tomatoes and shallots for about 5 minutes. Add the Madeira and sugar and simmer for 20 minutes. Purée in a blender or food processor and press through a strainer into a clean pan. Season to taste with pepper, add basil and bring the mixture to the boil. Cook until thick, then strain again. You should have 2 cups of purée.

Remove the mixture from the heat and stir in the eggs and the cup of cream.

Divide the mixture among 8 buttered timbale molds (don't fill to the top). Cover molds with buttered waxed paper and place in a large roasting pan. Pour in boiling water to a depth of ½-inch. Place the pan in a 400° oven and bake the timbales for 45 minutes. Remove the timbales from the water bath and set aside to cool.

Purée 1 to 2 avocados with lime juice to taste in a blender or food processor. Add enough cream to thin slightly. Place the lime mayonnaise in a pastry bag.

Spread 8 individual plates with avocado purée and unmold a tomato timbale in the center of each. Pipe several circles of lime mayonnaise around each timbale, feather and serve immediately.

Above: Tomato timbales with avacado purée
and lime mayonnaise
Right: Squid stuffed with scallop mousseline

SQUID STUFFED WITH SCALLOP MOUSSELINE

10 small fresh squid
¾ lb scallops
freshly ground pepper
Cognac to taste
lime juice to taste
1 whole egg
1 egg white
1¾ cups cream
for the stock:
3 cups white wine
3 cups water
3 tomatoes, chopped
1 bouquet garni
½ cup olive oil
lime juice to taste
to serve:
selection of salad leaves
roasted nuts
vinaigrette, preferably made with raspberry
    vinegar (optional)

Place the container of a food processor or blender in the refrigerator for at least 30 minutes to chill thoroughly. Clean the squid. Remove all the tentacles and set them aside with the side flaps. Wash the body sacs inside and out and dry them thoroughly. Wash and dry the scallops; if possible to obtain the coral, separate from the white and reserve.

Remove the food processor container from the refrigerator, add the white of scallop and purée. Season with pepper, a few drops of Cognac and lime juice. Add the whole egg and the egg white. Purée again. Add the cream with care. The mousseline must remain firm.

Fill a pastry bag with the mousseline, reserving 4 heaping tablespoons, and half fill each squid sac.

Place the scallop coral in the processor with the reserved mousseline and purée again. Add the pink mousseline through a pastry bag so the squid sacs are three-quarters full. Secure each top with a woodpick and return to the refrigerator.
To make the stock: place the squid tentacles and side flaps in a large saucepan with the white wine, water, chopped tomatoes and bouquet garni. Bring to the boil, then lower the heat and simmer for 30 minutes. Strain the stock into a roasting pan and stir in the olive oil and some lime juice to taste. Bring the stock to the boil in the roasting pan. Submerge the stuffed squid, cover and bake in a preheated 350° oven for 30 minutes. Cool in the stock and refrigerate overnight.
To serve: spread a selection of prime, washed salad leaves on a serving plate. Slice the squid into rings and arrange on the salad. Garnish with nuts (such as roasted macadamias). The squid may be dressed with a raspberry vinaigrette.

TARTELETS OF ONIONS AND RAISINS

½ lb package frozen puff pastry
for the onion/raisin filling:
¼ to ½ cup olive oil
about 40 shallots or small pickling onions,
    peeled
1 to 2 tablespoons sugar
about 40 seedless raisins
½ cup tomato paste
¼ cup red wine vinegar
¾ cup red wine

Thinly roll out the pastry on a lightly floured board and use to line eight individual tart tins. Refrigerate for 30 minutes then line with waxed paper and fill with dried beans.

Bake in a preheated 400° oven for 20 minutes. Remove the paper and the beans and return the tarts to the turned-off oven for about 10 minutes to allow them to dry out.
To make the filling: heat the olive oil in a heavy-bottomed saucepan and toss in the shallots. Sprinkle with sugar and cook, turning occasionally, until they begin to caramelize slightly. Add the raisins, tomato paste, vinegar and wine and simmer, uncovered, for about 30 minutes until the liquids have reduced and the onions are glazed. Spoon the filling into the warm tart shells and serve immediately.

STUFFED ROAST SQUAB WITH SAVOURY MOUSSE

8 squab
1½ cups wild rice
2 to 3 tablespoons oil for browning squab
mousse:
½ cup unsalted butter
1 green apple, peeled and chopped
6 shallots, peeled and chopped
1 lb duck livers, cleaned
freshly ground pepper
grated nutmeg to taste
2 tablespoons Madeira, muscatel, Cognac or
    Calvados
2 teaspoons chopped fresh herbs (parsley,
    chervil, thyme)
½ cup cream
marinade:
1 cup red wine
½ cup olive oil
2 tablespoons maple syrup
2 tablespoons light soy sauce
juice of 1 large lime
juice of 1 small piece fresh ginger, squeezed
    in a garlic press
sauce:
1 tablespoon olive oil
1 onion, chopped
1 carrot, chopped
1 bouquet garni
1 tablespoon peppercorns
2 cups red wine
2 cups water

Begin the preparation the day before you intend serving the squab.
First make the mousse: heat half the butter in a saucepan over low heat and sauté the apple and shallots. Add the duck livers, increase the heat to high and sauté until the livers are seared on the outside but still pink inside. Transfer the livers, apples and shallots to a food processor or blender, and flavor with pepper and nutmeg.

Add the Madeira to the saucepan and stir well to incorporate any pan scrapings. Stir in the herbs and add this liquid to the food processor. Let the mixture cool slightly, then purée it with the remaining butter and the cream. Transfer the purée to a bowl, cover and refrigerate until firm.

Bone the squab and cut off the wing tips. Set the carcasses aside and place the boned squab side by side in a large non-metallic dish. Mix all the marinade ingredients and pour over the squab. Cover and refrigerate overnight.

To make the stock for the sauce: place the olive oil in a roasting pan and add the flattened squab carcasses, together with the onion and carrot. Place the pan in a preheated 400° oven for about 1 hour or until the bones are well browned. Pour off as much fat as possible and then transfer the bones and vegetables to a large pan. Add the bouquet garni and peppercorns and pour in the wine and water. Add more water if necessary to cover the bones. Bring the liquid to the boil, then lower the heat and simmer for several hours until the stock has plenty of flavor. Strain into a clean bowl, cool and refrigerate overnight.

Next day, cook the wild rice in a large saucepan with 3 times its quantity of liquid (water, veal or game stock). Boil the rice for 30 to 40 minutes or until tender.

To cook the squab: while the rice is cooking, remove the squab from the marinade and pat them dry with paper towels. Reserve the marinade. Fill each squab with mousse and carefully sew each bird up. Heat the olive oil in a large frying pan and sauté the squab, 2 or 3 at a time, for about 5 minutes until browned all over. Transfer to a roasting pan. When all the birds have been browned, roast them in a preheated 450° oven for 12 minutes, basting several times with some of the marinade.

Meanwhile, remove the stock from the refrigerator, discard any fat on the surface and combine with remaining marinade. Bring to the boil and cook steadily until the liquid has reduced to about 1 cup and is quite syrupy. The sauce can be finished by molding with a little butter or diluting with cream.

Arrange the roast squab on a large heated platter with the rice and serve with steamed snow peas and small pastry shells filled with shallots and raisins. Pour the sauce into a sauce boat and hand around separately.

Below: Roast squab stuffed with savory mousse served with wild rice and snow peas

CHOCOLATE PECAN TORTE

1¼ cups pecans
5 oz semisweet chocolate, preferably imported
½ cup unsalted butter
½ cup sugar
6 egg yolks
8 egg whites
to serve:
3 oz semisweet chocolate, melted
chocolate curls (see Note) or grated chocolate
powdered sugar
crème Chantilly (recipe follows)

Butter, flour and line with buttered waxed paper an 8-inch round cake pan that is 3 inches deep. Hand chop the nuts in order to retain some texture. Chop the chocolate by hand or in a food processor but do not let it become powdery.

In a large bowl, cream the butter and sugar until light and fluffy. Add the yolks, one at a time, beating after each addition. Fold in the nuts and chocolate. In a copper bowl whisk the egg whites

until stiff. Fold ⅓ of the whites through the chocolate mixture to lighten it. Fold through the remaining whites with a light but firm hand. Pour the batter into the prepared cake pan. Set the cake pan in a roasting pan and pour in boiling water to come halfway up the sides of the cake pan. Bake in a preheated 400° oven for 40 to 50 minutes. The top will be firm to the touch. Cool the cake in the pan for 15 minutes before turning it out on to a flat platter. Cover with plastic wrap and store in the refrigerator.

To serve: cover the cake with the melted chocolate. Mark each serving with a large sharp knife before the chocolate sets. Pile the chocolate curls on top and sprinkle with a little powdered sugar. Serve with crème Chantilly or a home-made coffee or Grand Marnier ice cream.

Alternatively the cake may be split and filled with cream flavored with

Cointreau and powdered sugar to taste. Only attempt to split the cake after it has been refrigerated, as this cake has a dense moist texture.

Note: To make chocolate curls, spread melted chocolate on to a rimless baking sheet or marble slab and leave to set uncovered in a cool place. When set, scrape a sharp knife over the surface so that the chocolate comes off in long curls. Handle as little as possible.

CRÈME CHANTILLY

In a very cold bowl, whip 1¼ cups heavy cream with 1 tablespoon sugar or sifted powdered sugar and 1 scant teaspoon of vanilla sugar.

Above: Chocolate pecan torte

171

Chicken Fried in Paper
Rolled Egg Pancake with Pork Filling
Stir-fried Scallops with Snow Peas
Crab Foo Young
Shredded Beef with Bamboo Shoots
Quick-fried Bean Sprouts
Barbecued Spare Ribs
Fried Spicy Shrimps
Fried Rice

CHINESE BANQUET
FOR TWELVE

A traditional Chinese banquet for up to twelve people can be prepared with relative ease by one well-organized cook. Contrary to popular belief, Chinese food is not just thrown together in minutes. For a meal such as this you need to set aside a day to shop and then a day to chop and prepare all the different sauces. Of course, the cooking is done just before serving, but if all the ingredients are ready, this is not a trial.

The more guests the better when you are having a large banquet because it justifies the variety of dishes which makes the meal so interesting. Courses are worked out carefully so that there is a variety of seafood, red meat, vegetables and so on. Each dish is cooked individually and served one at a time. Rice is not brought out until towards the end of the meal; it is considered bad manners to serve it early on because the guests might suspect that you are trying to fill them up.

Red and green are popular colors in Chinese cooking and symbolize luck and long life. The opposite is true of white which is to be avoided because it symbolizes death.

Apart from the egg pancakes with pork filling (which can be served cold) and the barbecued spare ribs (which bake in the oven), none of the dishes requires more than a few minutes cooking before it is served.

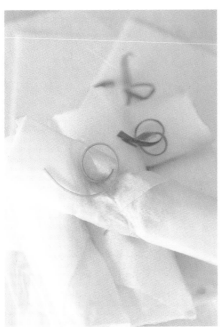

CHICKEN FRIED IN PAPER

1 lb chicken breasts, boned, skinned and sliced into bite-sized pieces
1 package rice paper
1 tablespoon shredded ginger
4 green onions, sliced thinly
oil for deep frying
marinade:
1 teaspoon light soy sauce
2 teaspoons oyster sauce
1 teaspoon sesame oil
1 tablespoon dry sherry
1 teaspoon sugar
¼ teaspoon salt
thin strips sweet red pepper to garnish

To make the marinade: combine all the ingredients in a large nonmetallic bowl.

Add the chicken pieces and let stand for at least 1 hour, stirring occasionally.

Cut the rice paper into squares, each measuring about 4 × 4 inches.

Place one or two pieces of chicken, a shred of ginger and a few slices of green onion in the center of a piece of rice paper and fold the flaps in, envelope fashion, to enclose the filling. Repeat with the remaining pieces of rice paper.

Heat the oil in a wok or deep-frying pan. When the oil is hot, fry the paper envelopes, eight at a time, for about 1½ minutes.

As they cook remove the envelopes with a slotted spoon and drain on paper towels. Serve hot, garnished with the red pepper strips.

Left and far left: Chicken fried in paper

ROLLED EGG PANCAKE WITH PORK FILLING
(Tan-Chuan)

4 eggs, beaten
1½ teaspoons vegetable oil
green onions to garnish
filling:
½ lb boneless pork shoulder, minced finely
1½ teaspoons soy sauce
1 teaspoon cornstarch
2½ teaspoons Chinese rice wine or pale dry
   sherry
¾ teaspoon salt
1 egg, beaten lightly

To make the filling: combine all the ingredients and mix thoroughly. Set aside.

Beat the 4 eggs together in a bowl. Set aside 1 teaspoon of the beaten egg to seal pancakes. Place a 12-inch wok or an 8-inch frying pan over moderate heat for 30 seconds. Coat the bottom of the pan with 1 teaspoon of oil. Pour in half the beaten eggs. Lower heat at once. Tip the pan from side to side until a thin, round pancake forms. Lift pancake and transfer to a plate. Using remaining oil, make the second pancake.

Spread half the pork filling over each pancake. Roll tightly like a Swiss roll and seal edges with the reserved beaten egg. Press edges firmly together.

To cook the pancakes: pour boiling water into the base of a steamer. Lay the pancakes on a heatproof dish ¾ inch smaller than the diameter of the steamer. Place on rack and cover steamer. Keeping the water at a slow boil, steam the pancakes for 20 minutes.

To serve: cut the rolls diagonally into ½-inch slices and serve hot, or refrigerate and serve cold, garnished with green onions.

Above: Rolled egg pancakes with pork filling

174

STIR-FRIED SCALLOPS WITH SNOW PEAS

½ lb scallops
¼ lb snow peas
2 tablespoons peanut oil
½ teaspoon grated fresh ginger
2 teaspoons cornstarch mixed with 1 teaspoon
   light soy sauce in ¼ cup water
½ teaspoon salt
chopped chives to garnish

Wash scallops in cold water; dry. Remove strings from snow peas. Heat the oil in a wok or frying pan and fry the ginger for 1 minute over high heat.

Add the scallops and stir for 1 minute. Add the snow peas and toss for another minute. Add the cornstarch mixture and cook, stirring constantly, until thickened, about 1 minute.

Sprinkle with salt and chopped chives and serve immediately.

CRAB FOO YOUNG

6 eggs
½ lb crabmeat, flaked and drained, sprinkled
   with 1 tablespoon sherry
½ teaspoon salt
5 tablespoons oil
¼ lb bamboo shoots, shredded
2 or 3 Chinese dried mushrooms, soaked,
   stems removed and shredded
⅓ cup peas
1½ cups chicken stock
1 tablespoon soy sauce
1 teaspoon sugar
1 teaspoon cornstarch, mixed to a paste with 2
   teaspoons water
to garnish:
crab claws
sweet red pepper strips

Beat the eggs lightly in a large bowl. Add the crabmeat and salt and stir well. Heat 3 tablespoons of oil in a wok or frying pan. Swirl oil around then pour the egg-crab mixture into the pan over high heat. When the center is set, turn over and fry other side. Slide on to a large platter and keep warm.

Add the remaining oil to the wok and sauté the prepared bamboo shoots, mushrooms and peas. In a bowl, mix together the chicken stock, soy sauce and sugar and add to the pan, stirring constantly. Add the cornstarch paste and cook, stirring constantly, until thickened. Pour this mixture over the "omelette" and serve immediately, garnished with red pepper strips and crab claws.

Above: Stir-fried scallops with snow peas
Left: Crab foo young

175

SHREDDED BEEF
WITH BAMBOO SHOOTS

1 egg white
1 teaspoon cornstarch
¼ teaspoon salt
½ lb flank steak, shredded
½ cup plus 3 tablespoons vegetable oil
1 clove garlic, minced
1 tablespoon fresh shredded ginger
5 red peppers, seeded and shredded
1 green onion, sliced thinly
¼ lb bamboo shoots, shredded
2 tablespoons wine
2½ tablespoons soy sauce
1 teaspoon sugar
1 teaspoon vinegar
a dash of sesame oil
green onion strips to garnish

In a shallow bowl, mix the egg white,
cornstarch and salt. Dip the shreds of
beef in this mixture and then fry slowly in
½ cup hot oil in a wok or frying pan over
low heat for 3 to 4 minutes or until the
meat is pale in color. As the shreds color,
transfer them to a plate with a slotted
spoon. Set aside.

Add the 3 tablespoons oil to the wok if
required, and when it is hot, sauté the
garlic, ginger, peppers, green onion,
bamboo shoots and beef over moderate
to high heat for 2 to 3 minutes. Sprinkle
with wine, stir in soy sauce, sugar, vinegar and sesame oil. Serve immediately,
garnished with green onion strips.

QUICK-FRIED BEAN
SPROUTS

3 tablespoons chicken fat or oil
1 tablespoon chopped green onions (or chives)
1 tablespoon chopped pickled cabbage (from
    Chinese food stores)
1¼ lb bean sprouts
1 8-oz can water chestnuts
1 teaspoon salt
3 tablespoons chicken stock
1 teaspoon sesame oil

Heat the chicken fat or oil in a large
saucepan over high heat. Add the onions
and pickled cabbage. Stir-fry for 30 seconds. Add the bean sprouts. Turn and
stir-fry briskly until all the sprouts are
well coated with fat. Add the water
chestnuts and sprinkle with salt. Continue to stir-fry for 1½ minutes. Add the
chicken stock and sesame oil, stir-fry for 1
minute more and serve.

Above: Shredded beef with bamboo shoots
Right: Barbecued spare ribs

BARBECUED SPARE RIBS

2 lb pork spare ribs
1 cup hoi sin sauce
to garnish:
shredded lettuce
chopped parsley, green onion or peppers

Two hours before cooking place ribs in a
single layer in a large nonmetallic dish.
Cover with hoi sin sauce and marinate,
turning occasionally.

Transfer the ribs, with their sauce to a
rack placed over a shallow roasting pan
and bake in a preheated 325° oven for
1½ hours or until tender. Baste with marinade while cooking. Serve on a bed of
shredded lettuce. Garnish with parsley,
spring onion or shredded peppers if liked.

FRIED RICE

2¾ cups rice
4 Chinese dried mushrooms
1 cup water
a dash of soy sauce
salt
a pinch of sugar
a dash of sesame oil
1 egg white
2 teaspoons cornstarch
6 oz boneless chicken, cubed
6 oz small shrimps, shelled
cooking oil for frying
2 eggs
1 tablespoon sherry
½ cup cooked peas
freshly ground pepper
½ cup chicken stock
sliced green onions, to garnish

Cook the rice. Drain and let stand for at least 1 hour. Soak the Chinese mushrooms in 1 cup of water until tender. Drain the mushrooms, reserving the soaking water. Remove and discard the mushroom stalks and cut the mushrooms in ½-inch squares. Mix the mushroom water with the soy sauce, salt, sugar and sesame oil. Set aside.

In a shallow bowl, mix the egg white with the cornstarch. Dip the chicken and shrimp in this mixture until coated. Heat a little cooking oil in a wok or frying pan. Remove the chicken cubes and shrimp from the cornstarch mixture with a slotted spoon and add them to the wok. Fry over low heat until they change color. Set aside.

Beat the eggs lightly in a small bowl. Add a pinch of salt. Heat 2 teaspoons oil in a small saucepan over moderate heat and add the eggs. Cook, stirring until scrambled.

Meanwhile heat 4 to 5 tablespoons cooking oil in the wok, add the reserved mushrooms, mushroom liquid, chicken and shrimps. Sprinkle with the sherry and 1 teaspoon salt, and sauté over medium heat for 1 minute.

Mix in the cooked rice and add a dash of pepper. Add the peas and scrambled eggs. Mix thoroughly over high heat for 2 to 3 minutes. Stir in chicken stock, and heat through. Transfer to a serving dish and serve hot, sprinkled with green onions.

Below: Fried rice
Bottom right: Fried spicy shrimp

FRIED SPICY PRAWNS

1 lb raw shrimps, shelled
oil for deep-frying
1 green onion, minced
1-inch piece of fresh ginger, minced
1 tablespoon wine
spicy mixture:
1 tablespoon brown bean sauce or 2 teaspoons
    Tabasco sauce
1 tablespoon tomato ketchup
1 teaspoon soy sauce
½ teaspoon salt
to garnish:
1 tablespoon sesame seeds
shredded green onions

First make the spicy mixture by combining all the ingredients in a bowl.

Wash the shrimps, remove tail tips and black veins. Cut into two or three pieces. Fry the shrimps in deep oil. As soon as they turn red, remove from the pan and set aside.

Carefully transfer 3 tablespoons of the hot oil to a clean frying pan and sauté the green onion and ginger. Stir thoroughly. Add the reserved shrimps and sauté quickly and thoroughly for 3 to 4 minutes. Sprinkle with wine and add the spicy mixture, stirring constantly over high heat for 2 to 3 minutes more, until done.

Serve the shrimps immediately, sprinkled with the sesame seeds and shredded green onions.

Cheese and Olive Tarts

Watercress Pasta with Mussels in Wine

Roast Suckling Pig with Raisin Stuffing
Orange Kumquat Sauce
Vegetable Gratin

Chocolate Hazelnut Soufflé
Rum-hazelnut Ice Cream

FORMAL LUNCH
FOR TEN

A formal lunch party, served outside, is a delectable way to celebrate a special occasion in summer. This inventive menu is influenced by classical European cuisine and makes the most of fresh seasonal vegetables. As guests arrive, offer around bite-sized cheese and olive tarts – they whet the appetite but still leave room for the courses to come.

Homemade watercress pasta makes an interesting change and is not difficult to make if you have a food processor and a pasta machine. The cooked pasta is tossed in butter and lemon juice with mussels that have been steamed in garlic and wine. As there is more to follow, make sure the helpings are not too large.

A suckling pig looks spectacular. Since a 30-pound pig is rather large for a domestic oven, the recipe dictates that it be cooked in sections in the oven and then reassembled. The pig's ears, nose and tail must be wrapped in foil to prevent burning and the pieces are stuffed with a fruity raisin stuffing. Citrus is a perfect flavor contrast to pork and so is utilized well in the orange kumquat sauce. As so much last-minute attention will be lavished on the pig, a simple vegetable gratin makes a good companion dish as it bakes in the oven and split-second timing is not essential.

Dessert is a triumph: a superb hazelnut soufflé served with home-made rum-hazelnut ice cream.

CHEESE AND OLIVE TARTS

3 sheets frozen puff pastry, thawed
5 oz tasty cheese, sliced
2 tomatoes, cut in small pieces
1½ cups large pitted black olives, quartered
a little grated Parmesan cheese

Grease individual tart pans. Roll out the pastry on a lightly floured surface. Cut the pastry, with a round pastry cutter, to fit the pans and place in the tart pans.

Cover each pastry round with a slice of cheese, a small piece of tomato and a quarter of an olive. Sprinkle with Parmesan cheese. Cook on the center shelf of a preheated 400° oven for 8 to 10 minutes until the pastry is golden brown.

Far left: Roast suckling pig with raisin stuffing (page 180): Vegetable gratin (page 181)

179

WATERCRESS PASTA WITH MUSSELS IN WINE

watercress pasta:
2 tightly packed cups watercress leaves
4 large eggs
4 egg yolks
1 teaspoon salt
5½ cups semolina, or more if necessary
mussels:
fresh mussels
2 cloves garlic, halved
2 cups dry white wine
to cook the pasta:
salted water
2 tablespoons oil
to dress the pasta:
3 tablespoons soft butter
⅔ cup olive oil
½ cup fresh lemon juice
reserved juice from steamed mussels
6 firm medium-sized tomatoes, peeled, seeded and chopped in ½-inch pieces
to garnish:
watercress
julienne (matchstick) strips of lemon rind

To make the pasta: place the watercress, eggs, yolks and salt in a food processor and process with an on/off action for 2 minutes, or until the mixture is puréed and pale green. Sprinkle the flour evenly over the egg mixture and process again with an on/off action until small beads form. If the dough is too moist, add more flour by the tablespoon until beads form. Remove the mixture from the food processor and place it in a plastic bag. Set aside for 15 minutes.

Divide the mixture into 4 before putting through the pasta machine, following the instructions of the manufacturer. Cut the pasta on a fettuccini roller. Leave to dry slightly before using.

To cook the mussels: wash them, remove and discard the beards and place the mussels in a large bowl. Cover with water and allow to stand for 3 to 4 hours, changing the water several times to clear the mussels of sand. Drain and place the mussels in a large saucepan with the garlic and wine. Cover the pan and steam the mussels over low heat until the shells open. Discard any that do not open. Remove most of the mussels from their shells, being careful to keep all the juice for the sauce. Leave 2 or 3 mussels per serving in their shells for garnish.

To cook and dress the pasta: boil a large pot of salted water, add 2 tablespoons oil, drop in the pasta and cook for 5 minutes. Drain well and return the pasta to the pot. Dress the pasta with the soft butter, olive oil, lemon juice and reserved juice from the mussels. Add half the shelled mussels and half the fresh tomatoes and toss well.

To serve: place the pasta-mussel mixture and sauce in a large bowl or platter, or divide into individual serving bowls. Garnish with the remaining mussels, tomato pieces, mussels in their shells and a little watercress and lemon rind.

ROAST SUCKLING PIG WITH RAISIN STUFFING

1 suckling pig, weighing about 30 lb
stuffing:
3 large onions
2 carrots, chopped
2 stalks celery, chopped
2 tablespoons parsley
1 pig's liver, cut in pieces
½ lb bacon, cut in pieces
½ cup butter
2 cups stale bread crumbs, moistened in milk
6 egg yolks, beaten lightly
4 tablespoons bread crumbs
freshly ground pepper
salt
nutmeg
3 tablespoons grated orange rind
1 cup raisins, soaked in port overnight
6 egg whites, beaten stiffly

Ask your butcher to cut the pig into 4 sections: head, forequarter, loin and hind legs (or 3 sections if the pig is smaller).
To make the stuffing: place the vegetables, parsley, pig's liver and bacon in a saucepan. Cover with a little water and add half the butter. Cook for 15 minutes then allow the mixture to cool. Mix in the stale bread and then transfer the mixture to a food processor or blender and process until well combined.

Melt the remaining butter and combine with the beaten egg yolks, bread crumbs, pepper, salt, nutmeg, orange rind and raisins. Combine with the meat and vegetable mixture. Lightly fold in the beaten egg whites.
To cook the pig: divide the stuffing between the forequarter, loin and hind quarters of the pig and secure with skewers or by stitching. Place the 4 sections in separate roasting pans and brush with oil (or, if your oven and roasting pan are big enough, place the sections in one dish). Wrap the pig's ears, nose and tail with foil to protect from the heat. Wedge a bone or something similar in the pig's mouth; it can be replaced by an apple when serving.

Place the roasting pans in a preheated 400° oven. Lower the temperature to 350° after 30 minutes. If your oven is not big enough to hold all the roasting pans at once, rotate them. The total cooking time per piece is 1½ to 2 hours.
To serve: assemble the cooked pig on a large platter by replacing the portions in their correct positions. Reserve the cooking juices and scrapings for the orange kumquat sauce (recipe follows).

Below: Watercress pasta with mussels in wine
Right: Chocolate hazelnut soufflé with rum-hazelnut ice cream

ORANGE KUMQUAT SAUCE

juices from the roasting pans used to cook the pig
2 cups orange juice
3 tablespoons grated orange peel
2 tablespoons brown sugar
kumquat marmalade, about 1 cup

Pour the cooking juices and scrapings from the pans used to roast the pig into one roasting pan. Add all the sauce ingredients. Reduce the sauce slightly, stirring thoroughly to combine the ingredients with the meat juices.

VEGETABLE GRATIN

4 onions, peeled and sliced
6 tablespoons olive oil
3 eggplants, sliced
1 clove garlic, crushed
½ lb mushrooms, sliced
salt
freshly ground pepper
3 lb zucchini, sliced
3 lb tomatoes, sliced
½ cup fresh thyme
½ cup freshly grated Parmesan cheese
bread crumbs

Brown the onions in 4 tablespoons of the olive oil. Add the eggplants, garlic and mushrooms. Season with salt and pepper to taste. Cook over a low heat, stirring occasionally, until all the vegetables have softened.

Place the cooked vegetables in the bottom of an earthenware dish. Arrange the sliced zucchini and tomatoes in rows on top and sprinkle with chopped fresh thyme. Sprinkle with salt and pepper and the remaining 2 tablespoons olive oil. Bake in a preheated 350° oven for 30 minutes.

Remove the dish from the oven, sprinkle with Parmesan and bread crumbs and bake for a further 15 minutes.

CHOCOLATE HAZELNUT SOUFFLÉ

8 oz semisweet chocolate
1¼ cups milk
½ cup sugar
6 egg yolks
2 tablespoons cornstarch
4 tablespoons cream
vanilla
8 egg whites
1 cup ground hazelnuts
extra butter and sugar for dishes

Butter 10 individual soufflé dishes and dust with sugar.

Melt the chocolate with half the milk in a heavy-bottomed saucepan. In a bowl, beat the sugar and egg yolks using an electric beater until thick and creamy. Mix the cornstarch with the remaining milk and gradually add to the egg mixture. Add this mixture to the chocolate mixture in the saucepan and cook over low heat until the mixture thickens and almost boils. Add the cream and vanilla.

Beat the egg whites until they hold stiff peaks. Fold the chocolate mixture into the egg whites. Pour the soufflé mixture into the prepared soufflé dishes, sprinkle ground hazelnuts over the tops and place the soufflés in a roasting pan. Add enough water to come halfway up the sides of the dishes. Cook on the center shelf of a preheated 350°F oven for 30 minutes.

Serve immediately with rum-hazelnut ice cream.

RUM-HAZELNUT ICE CREAM

8 large eggs, separated
1½ cups sugar
4 tablespoons rum
1½ cups ground hazelnuts
5 cups heavy cream
vanilla
½ cup sugar
chocolate leaves to decorate

Beat the egg yolks until creamy. Add the sugar and continue beating until the mixture is thick and creamy. Add the rum and ground hazelnuts and fold in with a spoon.

Beat the cream until stiff and add vanilla to taste. Beat the egg whites until they hold soft peaks. Gradually add the sugar to the egg whites, beating continuously until the mixture holds stiff peaks.

Gently fold the three mixtures together. Spoon into a container, cover and freeze. Serve with chocolate hazelnut soufflé and decorate with chocolate leaves.

Note: To make chocolate leaves, select large undamaged rose or bay leaves. Rinse and dry with paper towels. Brush the back of the leaves with a thin layer of melted chocolate. Allow to set and then apply a second coat. When completely set carefully peel off the leaves and set aside, uncovered, in a cool place until ready to use.

182

COCKTAIL PARTY
—FOR TWENTY—

Caviar Platter

Smoked Salmon and Shrimp Mousse

Smoked Salmon and Crab Rolls

Stuffed Mushrooms

Snail Croustades

Shrimp Barquettes with Quail Eggs

Caviar and Cream Cheese on Pastry

Zucchini Stuffed with Taramasalata

Melon and Prosciutto Rolls

Lobster Medallions

Jumbo Prawns with Dipping Sauce

Now that cocktail parties have made their comeback, canapés that are eye-catching, light and easy to eat with the fingers come into their own. This luxury line-up of food for a party of twenty fulfills all these requirements. The dishes can be prepared ahead of time and only require a little last-minute garnishing and reheating before the guests arrive. All but the shrimps and salmon mousse can be plucked straight from serving platters. By using different shaped cutters for the pastry bases your arrangements on the platters can be more striking. Variety is the key.

Slices of smoked salmon are filled with a blend of crabmeat, cream cheese, green pepper and mayonnaise; cooked shrimps and quarters of quail eggs are displayed on boat-shaped pastry bases; caviar and cream cheese top fluted ovals of pastry; and a rich snail mixture in baked bread croustades. Crisper options are baby zucchini stuffed with taramasalata and stuffed mushrooms or wrap small melon balls in slices of prosciutto.

Smoked salmon and shrimp mousse makes a good centerpiece for a table at a cocktail party. Even if most of the food is being handed around to mingling guests, it is good to have some food in a central position so that people can help themselves.

Left: Setting the scene for a cocktail party

CAVIAR PLATTER

Even a little caviar looks spectacular when served on a large bed of ice. Fill a large bowl with ice and place the bowl containing the caviar in the center. Fill four tiny bowls with chopped hard-boiled egg white, chopped hard-boiled egg yolks, finely chopped raw onion and sour cream. Arrange these around the caviar. Lay plenty of lemon wedges on the ice and decorate with salad burnet.

Pass around a bowl of toasted whole wheat fingers so that your guests can dip into a little of what they fancy.

Above: Caviar platter

SMOKED SALMON AND SHRIMP MOUSSE

shrimp mousse:
1 cup lemon mayonnaise
2 tablespoons lightly whipped cream
1 envelope gelatin, dissolved in 2 tablespoons brandy
½ cup chopped shrimps
2 tablespoons chopped chives
freshly ground pepper
smoked salmon mousse:
3 large slices smoked salmon, chopped
1 teaspoon lemon thyme
1 cup lemon mayonnaise
2 teaspoons lightly whipped cream
1 envelope gelatin, dissolved in a little hot water
garnish:
thin slices of smoked salmon to line mold
finely sliced lemon
sprigs of dill
aspic to glaze (optional)

Line a quart mold with slices of smoked salmon, it should come one-quarter of the way up the side of the mold.

To make the shrimp mousse: mix together the mayonnaise, whipped cream and dissolved gelatin. Fold in the shrimps and chives. Add salt and pepper to taste. Pour into the mold – the mixture should fill just over half of the container. Cover and refrigerate to set.

To make the smoked salmon mousse: blend together the smoked salmon, lemon thyme, mayonnaise, whipped cream and gelatin. The mixture will be pink. Add salt and pepper to taste. Pour into the mold on top of the shrimp mousse. Cover and refrigerate, preferably overnight, until set.

Unmold and garnish with sliced lemon and dill sprigs. Lightly glaze with aspic if liked.

Surround with additional smoked salmon slices if liked and serve.

STUFFED MUSHROOMS
(Makes 20)

4 cups water
juice of 1 lemon
20 fresh mushrooms
10-oz can clams, drained
salt
freshly ground pepper
Worcestershire sauce
2 tomatoes, peeled, seeded and diced

In a large flat pan bring the water and lemon juice to the boil, add the mushrooms and blanch them for 1 minute. Remove from heat, drain, and remove mushroom stalks. Arrange the mushroom caps, hollows up, on a flat serving dish or platter.

Place a frying pan over medium heat and add the clams. Season with salt and pepper to taste, add a sprinkling of Worcestershire sauce and, tossing the mixture well, cook for 3 to 5 minutes. Add the tomato pulp and cook for 1 minute more. Remove from heat and cool.

Put 1 teaspoon of the mixture into each mushroom cap and serve immediately. Alternatively, place the stuffed mushrooms on a lightly greased baking sheet and reheat for 10 minutes in a preheated 350° oven.

SMOKED SALMON AND CRAB ROLLS
(Makes 60)

1 teaspoon gelatin
2 teaspoons warmed Cognac
9–10 oz fresh crabmeat
¼ cup cream cheese, softened
1 tablespoon finely minced green pepper
2 tablespoons mayonnaise
salt
freshly ground pepper
a few drops of Tabasco sauce
1 lb thinly sliced smoked salmon cut into 60
small strips each measuring about
1 × 3 inches
15 slices thinly-cut brown bread, crusts
removed, cut in quarters (optional)

Dissolve the gelatin in the warmed Cognac. Mix the crabmeat, cream cheese, green pepper, mayonnaise and dissolved gelatin. Season with salt and pepper and Tabasco to taste.

Put 1 teaspoon of the crab mixture on each slice of smoked salmon, leaving a small rim at the top. Roll into small rounds. Place on a large flat tray, cover with plastic wrap and chill for several hours.

Serve the rolls as they are, or place them on the rounds of thinly sliced brown bread.

SNAIL CROUSTADES
(Makes 36)

To make the clarified butter for this recipe, heat salted or unsalted butter in a heavy-bottomed pan over gentle heat until melted but not browned. Remove from heat and allow the butter to stand for a few minutes. The water and nonfat solids will sink and with care you will be able to pour off the clarified butter from the top.

1 unsliced loaf of sandwich bread
¾ cup clarified butter
24 canned snails
½ cup dry vermouth
½ cup chicken stock
1 tablespoon minced green onion
1 teaspoon finely chopped fresh thyme
1 teaspoon finely chopped fresh tarragon
⅔ cup cream
2 tablespoons unsalted butter
2 tablespoons finely chopped Italian parsley
1 teaspoon brandy
salt
freshly ground black pepper

Remove the crusts from the loaf and cut it in 1-inch slices. Cut each slice in quarters. Using a serrated teaspoon (grapefruit spoon) or sharp knife, cut out a hollow in the center of each bread square, removing some of the crumbs, but taking care not to cut right through the bread. Arrange these croustades on a lightly oiled baking sheet and brush them with the clarified butter. Bake in a preheated 350° oven until croustades are golden. Transfer to a wire rack to cool completely.

Rinse and drain the snails. Chop them roughly and set aside. Place the vermouth, chicken stock, green onion, thyme and tarragon in a saucepan. Cook until the liquid has reduced to 2 or 3 tablespoons. Add the cream and reduce again until half the liquid remains. Add the snails and heat through. Stir in the unsalted butter, parsley and brandy and season with salt and pepper to taste.

Cool until set and spoon into the croustades. Serve immediately or place the croustades on lightly greased baking sheets and reheat for 10 minutes in a preheated 350° oven.

Left: Smoked salmon and shrimp mousse

PRAWN BARQUETTES WITH QUAIL EGGS
(Makes about 48)

pastry made from 1 package pie crust mix
cream cheese topping:
8 oz cream cheese, softened
2 tablespoons cream
a dash of Tabasco sauce
1 teaspoon sherry
1 teaspoon brandy
a dash of lemon juice
salt
freshly ground pepper
garnish:
12 hard-boiled quail eggs, shelled and
  quartered
48 cooked shrimps, peeled
sprigs of salad burnet for garnish

Roll out the pastry on a floured board to a neat rectangle. Arrange 12 barquette (boat-shaped) pans on a large baking sheet, lay the pastry over the pans and press the pastry into each pan. Gently

roll a rolling pin over the top of all the pans to cut away the excess pastry. Gather this together and use to line remaining pans in the same way. (Unless you have a large supply of barquettes you will have to bake several batches.)

Bake the barquettes in a preheated 400° oven for 12 to 15 minutes until pale gold. Ease the barquettes off the molds and carefully transfer them to a wire rack to cool completely.

Meanwhile mix the cheese, cream, Tabasco sauce, sherry, brandy and lemon juice in a bowl. Add salt and pepper to taste. Spoon the mixture into a pastry bag fitted with a large shell tip and fill each barquette with cheese mixture.

Add a quarter of a quail egg, 1 shrimp and a tiny sprig of salad burnet to each barquette and arrange them on a large tray to serve.

MELON AND PROSCIUTTO ROLLS

2 ripe medium-sized honeydew melons
½ lb lean prosciutto, sliced finely

Cut the melon in half crosswise and remove the seeds. Slice the melon across in 2-inch slices. Peel and cut into sticks about 2 inches long and ¼ inch square. Do this until you reach the curved ends of the melons and use these to cut out melon balls.

Trim the prosciutto of fat and cut into strips 2 inches wide. Place a melon stick at the end of a prosciutto strip and wrap round the melon 1½ times. Cut the prosciutto. Continue until all the melon and prosciutto have been used.

To serve: lay the melon and prosciutto rolls around the outer edge of a serving platter and pile the melon balls in the center.

CAVIARE AND CREAM CHEESE ON PASTRY
(Makes about 60)

pastry made from 1 package pie crust mix
Cream Cheese Topping (see previous recipe)
garnish:
1 3½-oz jar caviar
1 lemon, thinly sliced and cut in tiny wedges
fresh tarragon leaves

Roll out the pastry on a floured board and cut out small oval shapes with a fluted pastry cutter. Arrange the shapes on greased baking sheets and bake in a

preheated 400° oven for 10 to 12 minutes or until golden. Transfer to a wire rack to cool.

Meanwhile spoon the cream cheese filling into a pastry bag fitted with a large star tip. Pipe a little of the flavored cream cheese on to each pastry shape. Top the shapes with a little caviar and garnish each with a tiny piece of lemon and a fresh tarragon leaf. Serve immediately.

ZUCCHINI STUFFED WITH TARAMASALATA
(Makes 20)

1 7-oz can tarama, drained
4 slices day-old white bread, crusts removed
⅓ cup lemon juice
¼ onion, minced
1 clove garlic
1 envelope gelatin
⅔ cup olive oil
20 baby zucchini of even size

Soak the cod's roe in water to cover for 30 minutes. Soak the bread in a little water then squeeze dry.

Drain the cod's roe and place in a food processor or blender with the bread, lemon juice, onion, garlic and gelatin. Process until smooth. With the motor running, add the olive oil in a thin stream until the mixture is thick. Transfer to a bowl, cover and refrigerate for at least 2 hours.

Cut the zucchini in half lengthwise and scoop out the center with a tiny melon baller. Transfer the taramasalata to a pastry bag fitted with a large shell nozzle and pipe the mixture into the zucchini shells. Arrange the shells on a large platter and serve.

LOBSTER MEDALLIONS

Cut slices from cooked lobster tails and arrange on small circles of buttered bread.

Using aspic cutters, cut decorative shapes from thinly sliced truffles and lay one on each of the medallions. Top each with a tiny sprig of fresh dill and serve.

JUMBO PRAWNS WITH DIPPING SAUCE

Add crushed garlic to a well-flavored mayonnaise and place in a small serving bowl. Peel cooked prawns, leaving their tails intact. Place the bowl containing the mayonnaise in the center of a serving platter and arrange the prawns around it. Garnish with salad burnet and lemon slices and serve.

Above: Melon and prosciutto rolls
Right: A platter of canapés; from the right,
zucchini stuffed with taramasalata; lobster
medallions; stuffed mushrooms; shrimp
barquettes with quail eggs; snail croustades;
smoked salmon and crab rolls; caviar and
cream cheese on pastry

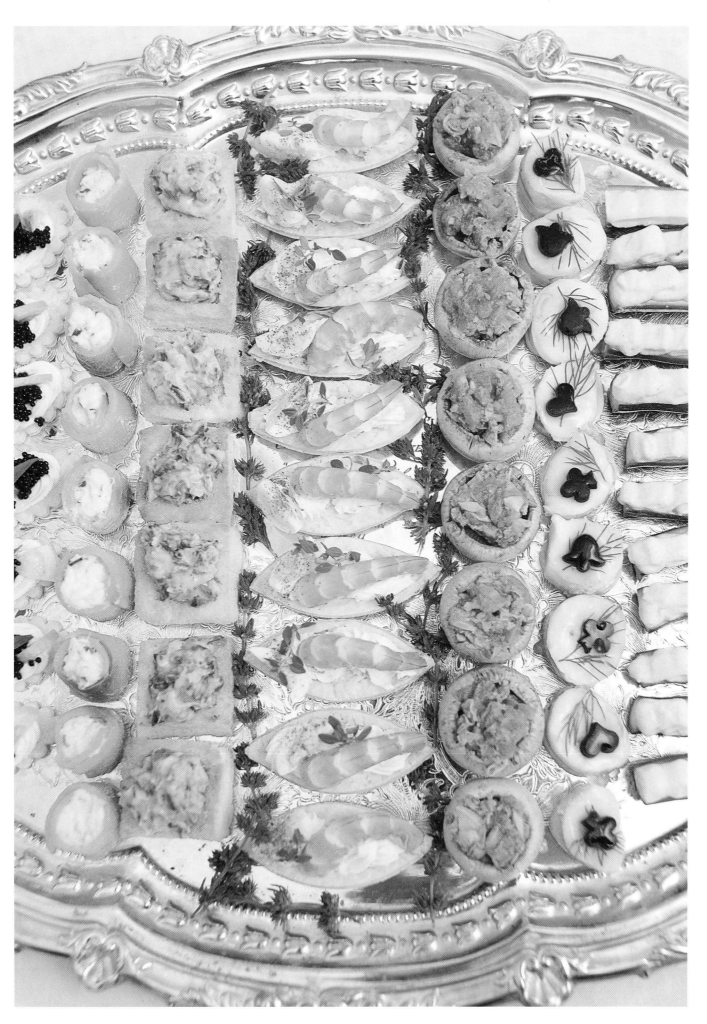

INDEX

A

Aïoli 50
Almond:
  Apricot soufflé with caramel almonds
    149
  Spiced almond chicken 92
Amaretto chocolate truffles 159
Anchovy sauce 153
Antipasto 123
Apple:
  Apple and pecan nut cake 39
  French-style apple tartelettes 42
Apricot:
  Apricot bavarois with peach-leaf
    sauce 119
  Apricot ice-cream 119
  Apricot soufflé with caramel almonds
    149
Aquavit 15
Artichoke:
  Artichoke hearts in sour cream 147
  Snow peas and artichoke salad 24
  Stuffed artichokes 124
  Stuffed artichokes with anchovy
    sauce 153
Arugula salad 137
Asparagus:
  Broad bean and asparagus medley
    119
  Sweetbread and asparagus tarts 32
Avocado:
  Brown butter salad 162
  Cherry tomatoes stuffed with
    avocado 22
  Guacamole 46
  Salad of romaine, avocado and quail
    eggs 28
  Tomato timbales with avocado purée
    and lime mayonnaise 168

B

Bacon:
  Bacon rolls 118
  Mushrooms sprinkled with sautéed
    bacon 42
  Pasta with bacon, mushroom and
    garlic sauce 144
**Bamboo shoots, shredded beef
  with 176**
Barbecued duck with noodles 140
Barbecued spare ribs 176
Bean:
  Beans flavoured with cinnamon and
    soy sauce 70
  Broad bean and asparagus medley
    119
  French beans with red pepper 132
  Refried beans 60

Bean sprout:
  Quail egg and bean sprout pyramids
    167
  Quick-fried bean sprouts 176
Beaujolais 14, 15
Beef:
  Fillet of beef with walnut stuffing 23
  Pan-broiled filets mignons 128
  Shredded beef with bamboo shoots
    176
  Spicy beef 69
Beet confits 88
Beluga caviar 97
Bentley (cocktail) 45
**Berry fruits with clotted cream
  and sugar bark 111**
Biscuits, herb 64
Blueberry soufflés 159
Brandied cheese 39
Brandied kumquats 89
Brandy 15
Brandy snap horns 89
Bread sauce 118
  Cardamom bread sauce 110
**Broad bean and asparagus medley
  119**
Brown butter salad 162

C

**Cailles à la Normande sur canapé
  98**
Cakes: *see also* **Desserts**
  Apple and pecan nut cake 39
  Chocolate cake 83
  Cinnamon crumb cake 61
Canapés, platter of 167
Cardamom bread sauce 110
Caviar:
  Beluga caviar 97
  Caviar and cream cheese on pastry
    186
  Caviar platter 184
  Egg pâté with caviar 36
Cestini con mascarpone 51
Champagne 14, 15
  glasses for 16, 17
Chapati 94
Chaudeau sauce 33
Cheese:
  Brandied cheese 39
  Cheese croutons 78
  Cheese and olive tarts 179
  Sesame cheese pastries 167
**Cherry tomatoes stuffed with
  avocado 22**
Chervil beurre blanc 114
Chicken:
  Chicken breasts stuffed with shrimps

  and baked in pastry 28
  Chicken fried in paper 173
  Chicken salad with honeydew melon
    and ginger mayonnaise 24
  Javanese chicken 69
  Oriental chicken 140
  Pineapple with chicken mayonnaise
    46
  Poached boned chicken 110
  Pollastrino alla diavola 75
  Rillettes of chicken 157
  Spiced almond chicken 92
China 16
**Chinese cabbage with garlic and
  ginger 70**
Chocolate:
  Amaretto chocolate truffles 159
  Chocolate cake 83
  Chocolate hazelnut soufflé 181
  Chocolate hearts with coffee anglaise
    and crème anglaise 107
  Chocolate pecan torte 171
  Date chocolate torte 47
  Tuiles with chocolate and violets 155
  Violet-topped chocolates 107
Cinnamon crumb cake 61
Cinnamon tea 95
Cocktails 45
Coconut:
  Coconut ice cream 141
  Hard-boiled eggs with spicy coconut
    sauce 70
  Poached tamarillo with coconut
    junket 115
Coffee:
  Coffee anglaise 107
  Pears in coffee syrup 79
  Spice islands coffee 70
Cookies:
  Butter cookies 149
  Cestini 51
  Melting moments 29
  Sfrappole 75
  Tuiles with chocolate and violets 155
Coral mayonnaise 105
Crab:
  Crab Foo Young 175
  Fresh crayfish with rice 46
  Smoked salmon and crab rolls 185
Cream cheese frosting 24
Creamy onions 39
Crème anglaise 107
Crème Chantilly 171
Crouton baskets 55
Croutons 113
  cheese 78
Cucumber raita 95
**Cucumbers stuffed with herb
  cheese 22**
Curry mustard sauce 97
Cutlery 17

189

ACKNOWLEDGEMENTS

Vogue Australia would like to thank the following for their invaluable contribution:
Margaret Cannon (Summer Country Lunch 21); Sandra and Bruce McLean (Poolside Gathering 27); Penny Bailey (Summer Lunch 31); Joanine Evans (Lunch on Board 35); Dominique Portet (Terrace Lunch 41); Jean Gardner (Riverside Dinner 45); Manuela Darling (Sunday Lunch Italian Style 49); Sandra Nicholas (Barbecue in Style 53); Sue Walker (Casual Brunch 59); Carolyn Lockhart (Huevos Rancheros 60); Joan Campbell (Casual Brunch recipe 61); Janet Alstergren (Country Lunch 63); Rupert Ridgeway (Indonesian Lunch 67); Lynne Mullins (Italian Medley 73); Guiliano Bugialli (Schiacciata con Ramerino 74); Joan Campbell (Warming Lunch 77); Claudia Thomas (Birthday Buffet Menu 81); Joan Campbell (Birthday Buffet recipes 82); Belinda Franks (Birthday Buffet recipes 83); Marieke Brugman, Howqua Dale Gourmet Retreat (Elegant Dinner 87); Lyn Hatton (Indian Feast 91); François and Ingrid Henry (Black Tie Dinner 97); Fiorella de Boos-Smith (Classic Italian 101); Ann Metzner (Teenage Dinner 105); Peter Seymour (Summer Dinner 109); Mark Armstrong (Gourmet Dinner 113) Joan Campbell (Formal Dinner 117); Margie Bromilow (Intimate Lunch 123); Carolyn Lockhart (Midweek Dinner 127 and Italian Supper 131); Trish and Julian Canny (Mediterranean Barbecue 153); Carolyn Lockhart (Oriental Supper 139); Jeffery Kitto (Stylish Lunch 143); Susie Kinnaird (Summer Picnic 147); Margaret Agostini (Celebration Lunch 153); Elise Pascoe and John Kelly (Dinner for a Summer Evening 157); Joan Campbell (Midwinter Dinner 161); Marieke Brugman, Howqua Dale Gourmet Retreat (Anniversary Dinner 161); Suelyn Grey (Chinese Banquet 173); Prue Fyfe (Formal Lunch 179); Kerry McManus (Cocktail Party 183).

Our thanks to the following publishers...
Macmillan (London & Basingstoke) and Alfred Knopf Inc for the use of Shrimp Brochettes. Adriatic style from 'The Classic Italian Cook Book', Marcella Hazan, translated by Victor Hazan, Copyright © 1973 by Marcella Hazan and Victor Hazan.
Angus & Robertson Publishers for the use of the Sorrel Sauce and Chaudeau Sauce from 'The Commonsense Book of Sauces' by Penny Bailey and Lindee Dalziell Copyright © Penny Bailey and Lindee Dalziell 1984.
William Collins Pty for the use of Weed Salad from 'Wild Food in Australia' by A B & J W Cribb, Copyright © 1974 William Collins, 1976 Fontana Books.

Photography
Grateful thanks go to the following photographers
Anthony Browell 165. **Michael Cook** 11; 16; 17; 30–33; 61; 112–119; 134–137; 156–159; 160–164. **John Hay** 15; 18–19; 26–29; 34–43; 52–55; 84–99; 104–111; 122–125; 166–171; 182–187. **Peter Johnson** 10. **Patrick Russell** 16; 146–149. **George Seper** 6; 8; 12; 14; 16; 44–51; 56; 58–60; 62–71; 76–83; 100–103; 120; 126–133; 138–145; 150–155; 172–181. **Rodney Weidland** 13; 72–75

Vogue Australia would also like to thank the following writers: Shona Martyn, Marion von Adlerstein, Betsy Brennan and Judy Pascoe.

Jacket Photograph
Photographed by George Seper
Styled by Carolyn Lockhart
Natural Store's marble used as a cheese and fruit platter with Villeroy & Boch's grey marblized buffet plate: gold Boda Nova knife and fork from Kosta Boda; white lace napkin handmade by Tonia Todman; flowers from Susan Avery. Woollahra, Sydney.